STRATEGIC COMMUNICATIONS FOR SCHOOL LEADERS

STRATEGIC COMMUNICATIONS FOR SCHOOL LEADERS

VICKI GUNTHER, JAMES MCGOWAN,
AND KATE DONEGAN

ROWMAN & LITTLEFIELD PUBLISHERS, INC.
Lanham • Boulder • New York • Toronto • Plymouth, UK

Published by Rowman & Littlefield Publishers, Inc.
A wholly owned subsidiary of The Rowman & Littlefield Publishing Group, Inc.
4501 Forbes Boulevard, Suite 200, Lanham, Maryland 20706
http://www.rowmanlittlefield.com

Estover Road, Plymouth PL6 7PY, United Kingdom

Copyright © 2011 by Vicki Gunther, James McGowan, and Kate Donegan

All rights reserved. No part of this book may be reproduced in any form or by any electronic or mechanical means, including information storage and retrieval systems, without written permission from the publisher, except by a reviewer who may quote passages in a review.

British Library Cataloguing in Publication Information Available

Library of Congress Cataloging-in-Publication Data
Gunther, Vicki.
  Strategic communications for school leaders / Vicki Gunther, James McGowan, and Kate Donegan.
    p. cm.
  Includes bibliographical references and index.
  ISBN 978-1-4422-0942-8 (cloth : alk. paper) — ISBN 978-1-4422-0943-5 (pbk.   ) — ISBN 978-1-4422-0944-2 (electronic)
  1. Communication in education. 2. Educational leadership. I. McGowan, James. II. Donegan, Kate. III. Title.
  LB1033.5.G87 2011
  371.2001'4—dc22
                                                                        2010047335

Printed in the United States of America

CONTENTS

Foreword by Roland S. Barth — vii
Preface — ix
Acknowledgments — xi
Introduction — xiii

Part I: Why Communication Is Important

1. The Public Has a Right to Know — 3
2. School Districts Need to Engender Trust — 13
3. School Districts Need to Advocate for Themselves — 25

Part II: How Best to Communicate

4. Know Who's Listening and How to Reach Them — 37
5. Align Communications with District Goals and Values — 51
6. Show, Don't Tell — 69
7. Cultivate Credibility — 77
8. Take Advantage of Technology — 85
9. Develop a Strategic Communications Plan — 97

Part III: It All Comes Together

10. What Happens When Your Communications Are Working — 111

Appendix 1: Communication Examples from District 73½ Education Fund Referendum in 2004	117
Appendix 2: Examples of Differentiating Communications	129
Appendix 3: Crafting the Vision	139
Appendix 4: Teacher-Family Communications	149
Appendix 5: Communications Audit	153
Notes	157
Bibliography	167
Index	173
About the Authors	179

FOREWORD

How many times, when working in a school, have we heard, "We have a communication problem around here." And how many times has little been done to successfully address the problem? Too many, I'm afraid.

The murky swamp that encompasses good communication often seems all but impenetrable to school people and to those who would assist them. In this tidy little volume, you will find the heroic effort by three of those school people to describe, analyze, and address the issue of communication in our beleaguered field. Abundant examples from successful practice, conveyed in clear and accessible prose, bring a fine grain to the discussion.

If there is more to be said about good communication, I'm not sure what it might be. This rich compendium of research and helpful ideas says it all—and with the insight that only veterans of the school world can know, understand, and explicate.

But introducing the healthy practices described here into the culture of a school or a district will not be easy. Transformation of "the way we do things around here" will require a will and a willingness to lead from the central office, principals, and teachers alike.

Further, it will not suffice for a school community to communicate directly and frequently about the consequential affairs of daily school living such as schedules, committees, and meetings. The real challenge to those who would bring rational, transparent communication to the schoolhouse lies in discussing the "nondiscussables": in educators having the honesty, clarity, and directness to confront inflammatory issues such as equity of workload, teacher evaluation, the underperforming educator, racism, and compensation. Addressing these endemic, frequently debilitating, corrosive, and crucial school matters is not only a matter of developing skill, timing, and ingenuity. Really good school communicating will never prevail until we educators muster qualities that too often lie dormant within us: decency and, above all, courage. Sadly, no book can summons these qualities. We will have to call them forth, ourselves.

Strategic Communications for School Leaders offers a vital beginning to this quest. Enjoy and be enriched by this "required reading." I have.

Roland S. Barth, educator

PREFACE

The book you're about to read is the result of more than a year of work but is also the product of years of labor in the vineyards of public education. During our time working together, we—a current school superintendent in her first top job, a former principal and superintendent-turned-academic, and a former board president with years of experience as a reporter, editor, and consultant—began initiatives, conducted campaigns, managed small crises, and did the day-to-day work of running a school district.

All the while, we kept coming back to the notion that communication was a key component of whatever we tried to do. When we communicated well, we had success—winning a property tax referendum, getting a needed addition built, and keeping our parents and other community residents informed about what their schools were doing and involved in their activities. When our communication was poorly thought out or not well executed, we didn't have such positive outcomes and had to spend even more time clarifying, revising, and trying to inform and persuade.

Because the focus of our efforts came back so often to communication, it eventually dawned on us that we might have things to say that others in the field would find useful—particularly given our differing roles (veteran administrator, younger administrator, and board member). That led us to make presentations at national educational conferences about why and how school leaders should think strategically about communications. When Patti Belcher, acquisitions editor at Rowman & Littlefield, suggested we pursue our presentation topic further with a book, we agreed. So here we are.

As we looked deeper into literature and practice on effective school communications, we found much valuable work by others. Their work is referenced herein, and we hope you find those references useful.

Because this book arose from our own work and experience, it is focused on practice, and our intent is to talk directly to practitioners. We're writing for decision makers who set policy and establish procedures and expectations throughout an education organization. Those include superintendents and other top administrators, principals, school communication managers or directors, board members, and those who aspire to be administrators and are reading this text for a course in an educational administration degree program. Teachers, support staff members, and key community supporters may benefit from this book as well. Educators may not have formal training in communication, but we're sure they recognize how important it is to the welfare of their schools and districts.

We frequently refer in this book to the district's decisions or the district's need to communicate. When we mention "district" or "school," it is typically shorthand for the leaders who guide a district's operation, or the district as an institution within its larger community.

We encourage you to consider your own circumstances and experiences as you read. We hope our words will resonate and that you will find both broad and specific meaning and value in what we have written.

ACKNOWLEDGMENTS

We would like to express our deep appreciation to the family members, friends, and colleagues who became the "community" from which this book springs. Without their help, this could not have been written.

We are especially grateful to Fred Brill, Kai Conway, David Donegan, Julia Haley, Ted Purinton, and Dick Streedain for taking the time to read and comment on prior drafts. Their insightful criticism made this a better book.

We also want to thank those who shared their experiences in interviews, including Jeff Arnett, Robert Avossa, Carlos Azcoitia, Fred Brill, Kelly DeFeciani, Julia Haley, Linda Hanson, Trinette Marquis, Frank Porter, Griff Powell, Ed Rafferty, Nancy Stewart, Dick Streedain, Linda Tafel, and Jim Ylisela. We appreciate their generosity.

We owe a special debt of gratitude to Jim Yarnall, whose research assistance, patient editing, and careful proofreading saved us from countless mistakes, and Sharon McGowan, a superior editor who determinedly kept us focused on writing a coherent, comprehensible narrative. She reminded us again and again that it's the writers who should suffer, not the readers. Whatever is clear and understandable in this book is due in some measure to her efforts; whatever is not is solely the fault of the authors.

We are also grateful to the editors and staff at Rowman & Littlefield, who not only have given us the opportunity to share our ideas and arguments with an audience but have also skillfully guided a trio of neophytes through the unfamiliar journey of publishing a book.

Lastly, we are extraordinarily grateful to Roland Barth for his thoughtful foreword and for his generous advice as a thinker, writer, and educator. We are longtime admirers of his work, and we value his contribution most highly.

INTRODUCTION

> Everything that our organization does—and sometimes what we don't do—sends a message.
>
> —Twin Rivers Unified School District[1]

Every individual communicates, through words, expressions, gestures, attitudes, and actions. Every organization communicates, through the words and actions of its leaders and workers, and through its formal and informal means of information distribution.

Because communication is constant and pervasive, it can be taken for granted or, at least, not considered worthy of the same care and attention that school leaders devote to other aspects of their jobs. As college basketball coach Bob Knight famously said in showing his contempt for sportswriters, "All of us learn to write in the second grade. Most of us go on to greater things."[2]

Knight, of course, eventually left coaching to become a communicator himself, as a television broadcaster. But there's little doubt that many share his conviction that communication skills and tools pale in comparison to other, "greater things."

We beg to differ. In our view, communication supports everything that schools do. In the same way that literacy and social and emotional skills underlie all the learning activities that students engage in, so communication underlies the efforts of schools to train and manage staff members, teach students, handle finances, run facilities, and build and maintain public support. But because communication seems to be everywhere—and to always have been there—it's easy to lose focus on the who, what, when, where, how, and why of it.

And that's why we wrote this book. We've taken a step back and looked deeply into the communicating that schools do, from mundane hallway signs to glitzy Web graphics and video. We've laid out the reasons communications are important and the means by which they can be accomplished. In putting this together, we've borrowed liberally from our own experiences—not because we hold ourselves up as paragons but rather because of what we've learned from our varying perspectives as a veteran school administrator, a new superintendent, and a board member who is a professional communicator. We've also reviewed the work that others have done in the field of communications in general (and school communications specifically), examined the practices of schools across the country, and learned from their experiences and perspectives. We think we've extracted insights that practitioners anywhere can identify with, reflect upon, and take value from.

One overarching lesson we've learned is this: the quality of your communications depends largely on the core values of your school or district and its leaders. Those values (and the attitudes and behaviors that result from them) affect what you expect your communications to accomplish, how they are executed, and how they are perceived and understood. No matter how skilled you may be, you can't communicate values you don't hold.

This book isn't a manual showing how to spin, shift blame, or lie. We argue for what we believe to be the hallmarks of top-notch school communications—honesty, credibility, thoroughness, careful planning, skillful execution, evaluation, and revision. To repeat—we believe that communication supports every aspect of school or district activities and is just as important as any other endeavor.

At the same time, we recognize that communication is not the only objective school leaders have. There are times when the less said, the better—in the name of protecting student or staff privacy, or during sensitive negotiations, to name two examples. But the fact that communications can sometimes hurt your cause—statements made without sufficient context or spur-of-the-moment comments you wish you could take back—only reinforces the notion that communications have to be fully considered before they take place. To be effective, they have to be planned carefully and executed well.

WHO SHOULD READ THIS BOOK

We believe anyone in a school leadership role can benefit from this book. That includes superintendents, administrators, board members, teachers, and community leaders. We also think there is benefit to districts across all dimensions—large and small; affluent and poor; urban, suburban, and rural; public and private; with a communications staff and without.

We hope you will view the themes, examples, and recommendations in this book through the lens of your own experience. We encourage you to look closely at what you're already doing, think about whether there are things that need to be improved, and see whether we provide a new idea to try or a new slant on your practices. We want to inspire you to think deeply about how communication and school leadership affect each other, as well as offer concrete suggestions that could be put into action quickly.

To reach these ends, we tell stories. Whether they are our own or those others have told us, we think the lessons they portray apply across the spectrum of American schools. We think they will help our readers reflect on their own circumstances and values, learn from the experiences of others, and activate the process described by Roland Barth, founder of the Harvard Principals' Center: "It is only when the story about practice is accompanied by analysis that the narrative is transformed from war story into craft knowledge."[3]

WHO WE ARE

First, here is a bit of background: Our career paths crossed in Elementary School District 73½ in Skokie, Illinois, a suburb immediately north of Chicago. District 73½ covers a slice of an "inner-ring" village that straddles the line between urban and suburban; the population of both the municipality and the district grew in the post–World War II boom, declined in the 1970s and 1980s, and became much more diverse in the past two decades. District families report more than sixty different languages are spoken at home, and the proportion of students requiring English-language instruction and financial assistance has increased steadily. Experienced educators know that changes such as these affect schools, teachers, and administrators; as we point out later on, we believe they affect school communications as well.

Each of us brought our own values and experiences to the district and to this book. Vicki Gunther grew up in Chicago, served as an administrator and principal in the Chicago Public Schools, was both a principal and superintendent in District 73½, and remains vitally involved in the field of education through her teaching at National-Louis University. Her two sons are grown. Kate Donegan grew up in rural Illinois; both of her parents are educators, and she's risen quickly in the family business, moving from special education teacher to assistant principal to principal to superintendent in little more than a decade. She has three boys under age 7 and lives in the district. James McGowan also grew up in Chicago, worked as a newspaper reporter covering schools and local government, and worked for school districts and education organizations through his communications firm. He sat on the district's elected school board for eight years, five as president. Both his daughter and son graduated from district schools.

We know we're not the only ones thinking about school communication, and we're well aware that many school leaders do the things we discuss in this book very well—and may do them very differently than we might in the same circumstances. The research we've done has shown us that a great many educators are committed to communicating well and are finding ever more innovative ways to do so. We've learned much from them.

But as you'll see, we've drawn extensively upon our school service and tried hard to reflect upon its relationship to communication. It's in large part because our experiences are not unusual but typical that we believe others can extract value from what we have to say. The point is, it's not about us—it's about anyone in a similar position throughout American education.

HOW THE BOOK IS STRUCTURED

In each chapter, we discuss a theme related to good school communications. There are ten:

1. Communication with the public is both an obligation and an opportunity for schools.
2. Schools need the community's trust, and building trust requires communication.
3. Through communication, schools make the case for public support.
4. Schools must understand their audiences and their means of communication.
5. Good school communications flow from goals and values—and exemplify them.
6. Good communications—particularly good examples and stories—draw the community closer to the schools.

7. School communications must be credible to be effective.
8. Wise use of technology allows schools to reach people more effectively, more often.
9. The best school communications are planned; the best plans rely on research, analysis, smart implementation, evaluation, and revision.
10. Schools that communicate well are rewarded, because all their stakeholders are engaged in their work.

At the end of chapters 1–9, we review key ideas, encourage you to reflect upon relevant practices that you already use, and suggest practices that you might try if your district is not already doing them.

We realize that books aren't really built to be interactive. We would like to open up a continuing conversation by inviting you to share your reactions, criticisms, practices, and insights at our website, www.strategiccommunications4schools.com/. We plan to contribute regularly there and will keep it going as long as interest warrants.

To sum up, our readers will learn

- why schools must communicate (to satisfy the public's right to know, to build trust, and to advocate);
- the importance of understanding the different audiences within a school community, displaying the goals and values that underlie communications, communicating credibly, and using technology well;
- how crucial it is to plan, evaluate, and revise communications; and
- that communications, as important as they may be, are only a means to an end—that of building a true and lasting school community.

Part I

WHY COMMUNICATION IS IMPORTANT

1

THE PUBLIC HAS A RIGHT TO KNOW

Communication with the public is both an obligation and an opportunity for schools.

A free society is maintained when government is responsive and responsible to the public, and when the public is aware of governmental actions. The more open a government is with its citizenry, the greater the understanding and participation of the public in government.

—New York State Freedom of Information Law[1]

Every leader in the realm of public education is aware of the burden of disclosure. Budgets are published in the local newspaper or online; test scores (for better or for worse) provide fodder for the media and pundits; and meetings and deliberations must take place in public, and in some states, closed sessions must be recorded just to prove no laws were broken.

But we're here to argue that openness and honesty are really not a burden; rather, they are values to be embraced by school leaders everywhere. Districts whose sole goal is to do the minimum—comply with applicable laws and parcel out any other information as though it required high-level security clearance—miss the point. In a world of shrinking resources, an ever more demanding public, and a growing number of options for discriminating families (including private schools, charter schools, and homeschooling), communication is imperative.

Consider a few questions. How does your district win community support when needed? How does it build trust? How do you tell people about the good things happening in your schools every day? How do you break bad news?

School leaders who believe that "honesty is the best policy" answer our questions differently than those who believe that "what they (parents, students, staff members, or the community) don't know won't hurt them." If you're one of the latter, we're betting that, when the referendum comes (or the bitter board election, or public fight over curriculum, or some other crisis), what they don't know could hurt *you*. There can even be occasions when efforts to withhold information actually cost districts money (see box below).

> There are real costs attached to the choice *not* to communicate. In 2005, a district in Chicago's west suburbs declined a request from a school board candidate to reveal details of its superintendent's employment contract, on privacy grounds. Four years later, the Illinois Supreme Court ruled the district had to make the contract public. Cost to the district: more than sixty thousand dollars in legal fees. In addition, the Illinois attorney general cited the case in her efforts to strengthen the state's public records law, which would likely increase the regulatory burden on all of the state's public bodies—including school districts.[2]

We say that the ideal answer to the questions posed above is "through carefully planned and executed communications." We'll get into the details later, but we strongly believe that a successful district must have a good strategic communications plan and that the plan has to be supported by a commitment to *more* communication rather than *less*, *openness* rather than *secrecy*, and a determination to *listen* as well as to *talk*.

Many school leaders are leery of doing more than the minimum. Rich Bagin, executive director of the National School Public Relations Association, has noted, "Most school leaders have not been nurtured in [the concept of] transparency. . . . They fear practices that promote openness might undermine their power and position, give fuel to special-interest groups with opposing agendas or simply consume too much time."[3] There could certainly be circumstances under which those fears come true, but openness has its benefits as well. As researcher Megan Tschannen-Moran has observed, "When leaders make themselves vulnerable through these forms of openness, a spiral of trust is initiated that serves to foster increasing levels of trust in the organization."[4]

We'll talk more about trust in the next chapter. In this one, we will talk about what you *have to* tell people and what you should *want to* tell people. Your district already has the means in place to develop rich and meaningful communications, since you use the same communications tools to do the minimum as you would to go beyond. Deciding what you want to tell people can help you think about not only *what* you want to say but also *how* and *why*. And those are critical to solid strategic planning—whether you're planning communications or mapping out your district's overall goals and objectives.

FINANCIAL REPORTING

You already know how much time, paper, PowerPoint slides, newsprint, and Web space your district's financial reporting chews up. You also know how your financial reporting process is prescribed by law or regulation—requiring you to publish budgets, hold public hearings, reveal the details of purchases in board meeting minutes, and much more.

All that stems from the public's right to know and taxpayers' desire to hold you accountable for how their money is spent. Because of its very nature as a set of rote requirements, though, much financial reporting becomes routine, even boring, both for your district and your community. How many people ever read your budget? How closely do outsiders scrutinize your purchases? We suspect your answers are not many and not very.

But failing to provide clear and detailed explanation—putting your district's financial decisions in full context—is a missed opportunity. By explaining not only *what* your district is spending its money on but also *why*, and *how* it arrives at those decisions, you build trust. By being open and inclusive and actively seeking informed input from members of the community (year in and year out, not just at referendum time), you build consensus. Trust and consensus lead to support for your entire enterprise and help you promote engagement.

Here's how your district can go beyond the minimum. Don't just release the budget; talk about your process. Who's involved? How long does it take? What criteria do you use to decide whether to undertake (or extend or eliminate) an initiative? How do you judge whether a program is worth what's being spent? Answers to questions such as these provide details that add up to a larger message—that the district makes its financial decisions carefully, based on reason, experience, core values, and hard data.

> Time is a scarce resource, and its allocation affects all the work that schools do. This has two obvious implications for school communications—leaders must find the time to communicate effectively, and members of the school community must find the time to receive messages. While we contend throughout this book that communication should be a high priority and get the attention it deserves, we're well aware that leaders are stretched thin and audiences are wary of information overload. Good communications planning should take both of those concerns into account.
>
> "Communication takes time. Too often, school leaders are unable or unwilling to devote the time necessary for proper communication," writes Douglas J. Fiore, a former principal and now education professor at Virginia State University. But he argues that it's time well spent: "The mistakes that so often occur when individuals rush through the communication process often lead to taking more time to fix problems caused by their hurrying in the first place. Taking the time to communicate purposefully and carefully in the beginning saves time in the long run."[5]
>
> Regarding information overload, there's no denying that people in your community have busy lives, may feel overwhelmed by the number of messages they receive daily, and might be turned off if they believe your district is contributing to their burden. This is why it's critical that your district understands its audiences and knows what information each one needs and how it should be sent (see chapter 4); uses technology wisely (see chapter 8); and communicates "purposefully and carefully," as Fiore recommends (see chapter 9).

Your district can go even further. Explain where the money comes from. Discuss how taxes are levied and collected. Give taxpayers information that allows them to fairly judge the job you're doing. Explain what's in the district's control (property tax levy, for example) and what isn't (property tax assessment), and how what's not in your control affects what is available to spend. Put your tax levy in context: How has it changed over time? How does it compare to that of your neighboring districts? What factors explain the differences? How do those factors reflect on the quality of your stewardship?

Besides taxes, your district may have other sources of revenue—fees, government grants, or foundation assistance. Explain how these work. If your district actively pursues grant money, discuss your successes (and failures). Talk about the funds raised by the district and its affiliates (Parent-Teacher Association [PTA], foundation, band supporters, athletics boosters, etc.) and why. Make clear that those fundraising efforts enable precious tax resources to be channeled directly to teaching and learning. Marshal every detail you can to support the message that your district is penny wise and pound prudent.

You can add credibility to this message by making clear how, and how well, your financial reporting is done. Explain how you arrive at your financial projections. If you submit to yearly audits, publicize the results. Even a critical auditor's report makes the point that your district's books are open to public view. While a completely clean report is probably the best news, an auditor's recommendation for changes in your process provides a future opportunity to reinforce the concept that you are committed to transparency and continuous improvement. If your state rates your district's financial performance, discuss that, too. Good, bad, or indifferent, it's an opportunity to explain what you're doing and why and to demonstrate that you aren't hiding anything.

STUDENT AND STAFF DATA

Most, if not all, districts report certain demographic details about their students (such as race, language status, and eligibility for free or reduced-cost lunches), as well as information about teachers (average salaries, experience, and qualifications) and other basic data (teacher-student ratios and administrator-student ratios). An experienced observer might be able to draw some conclusions about your district from bits of information such as these; most members of your community likely cannot.

But a fuller description of your students and staff members (and how the demographics are changing, if they are) can help tell your community a story worth telling. For example, an increase in non-English-speaking families in the district would have implications for your staffing patterns, as well as overall teaching and learning. You may be very proud of the way your students and staff members handle diversity; you may also have to allocate your limited resources very differently than your predecessors did to address the challenges posed by multiple languages and cultures.

Those are issues worth explaining, particularly to community members who no longer have a direct connection to your schools. For many, the mental picture of what happens in your school buildings is frozen in time—at a point when their children were in school, or even when they themselves attended. The more things have changed, the more important it is for you to explain what's changed and what it means for your budget, for your test scores, and even for the content your students are expected to master.

For those most closely tied to your daily work, there are additional reasons to communicate clearly about changes in your population. You want your students to know because dealing with diversity will become part of the subject matter of their school lives and because they will play a role in welcoming and acculturating newcomers. You want your families to know because they, too, will play a welcoming role; but you also want them to be aware that—in the zero-sum game of allocating limited resources—having to spend more in one area (addressing needs of non-English speakers, for example) means having less to spend in others. While it's up to school leaders to make the tough budget decisions related to an issue such as this (i.e., cut spending in one area while increasing it in another, or seek to generate more overall revenue by raising taxes or fees), they can build support for their decisions by sharing with their stakeholders their priorities, the data they use to make their decisions, and the effects their decisions have on teachers and students—and by listening and taking into account the feedback they receive when they do so.

Having to make these tough decisions may pose serious problems for school leaders, such as the potential for pitting one segment of the community against another. In our hypothetical example above, you could find yourself answering to those who believe their children are losing out because "outsiders" are moving in. In such a case, conflict may be unavoidable—but your district will be in a better position to get past it if the community has the facts and can appreciate the district's situation. However difficult the conflict may be, withholding communication isn't likely to help.

You're not likely to win total agreement with every decision your district makes, but delivering the full story to all interested parties is the first step in trying to win consensus—on the best ways to spend only what you have, to seek more revenues, or both. Good communications don't guarantee that you'll reach consensus, but they lay the groundwork for it.

Similarly, your district doesn't want to allow raw information about the salaries, credentials, and experience of its teaching staff to hang out

> School districts' financial decisions often draw public notice, and even some protest. But curricular decisions can come under fire, too. In spring 2009, a suburban Chicago district had to answer a challenge from some parents to a book on its high school summer reading list. The district neither ignored nor caved into complaints. The district chose not to strike the book from its list (which always had included alternatives to the book in question), but it also formed a committee, including parents, to review future summer reading assignments. The committee gives parents a voice and gives school leaders a chance to listen.[6]

there unexplained. There's a "good news, bad news" scenario about key characteristics of your teaching staff; a deeply experienced group of long-time teachers, for example, comes with a higher price tag than does a less-experienced cohort. You want to clearly state truths about your staff in ways that are not argumentative and provide clear context. Veteran teachers may come with higher salaries and may (in some cases) be less willing to embrace new technologies or methods, but their experience with your curriculum and your community offers real benefits. They may get more done in less time than an inexperienced staffer who's still learning how to command a classroom, adjusting to your preferred methods, or understanding your student body.

STUDENT ACHIEVEMENT

Information about student achievement is in greater demand than ever. The No Child Left Behind Act (NCLB) and its regulations have shone a hot spotlight on test scores and their ramifications, but families and communities have always cared about how well their students are doing. One of the most far-reaching impacts of NCLB has been to narrowly define the discussion about what constitutes achievement—focusing public attention on test scores to the exclusion of nearly everything else.

And regardless of how you view those scores, you're duty-bound to present them annually. The real test of whether you're communicating as well as you should lies with what *else* you're saying about achievement. For starters, your district can confront the issue head-on by discussing all

> Beware of unintended consequences in communicating about student achievement. Writer Maura Casey observed that her child's district's efforts to give families more information about how students were doing were thwarted by the district's obfuscatory language. She noted, "If schools don't offer information that is simple, they will end up creating more barriers, especially in cities like Hartford where many of the students come from families where English is not the first language. If report cards are weighed down with educational jargon that even native English speakers have to struggle to understand, it is fair to ask, who are the administrators really reporting to: students and their families or the educational bureaucracy?"[7]

the ways it assesses student progress—standardized achievement testing, performance-based assessment, in-class and homework assignment grades, and portfolios of student work. Further, you can explain how a range of assessment tools provides a clearer, more well-rounded picture of achievement than any single tool could.

And your district can go further. Show off stellar examples of student work. If student art is displayed at the village hall or town library, let people know. Publicize student awards (and staff awards, for that matter). If your older students mentor younger ones, or your outstanding students tutor their peers, promote those programs as well. This anecdotal evidence of achievement paints the telling details in your overall picture—and because these are real-life examples of what's actually happening with children and families, your community members will respond well to them. On the Web page pictured in figure 1.1, teachers at Lake Mills Community School in Iowa explain and illustrate a physics assignment and relate it to real-world engineering problems.[8]

In all of the instances discussed in this chapter, it's important to remember that your expertise as a school leader, combined with your experience within the district, gives you knowledge and information that your constituents don't have. While it's not possible (or desirable) to share every possible detail with everyone, you'll derive real benefit from offering clear, detailed explanations of your work, your decision making, and your students' progress.

Sometimes this means discussing things you believe to be elementary or that are so deeply ingrained in the daily routine that you seldom think about them. Before you begin to communicate—in person, on paper, or online—put yourself in your readers' or listeners' shoes. What don't they

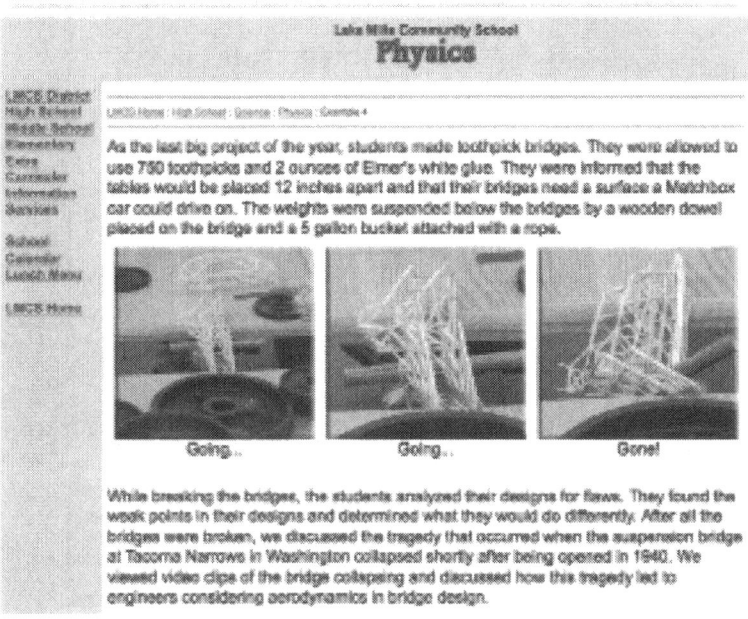

The Public Has a Right to Know 11

Figure 1.1. A classroom physics project at Lake Mills Community School in Iowa takes on real-world ramifications.

know? What do they need to know? What details would put this issue in context? What example would drive this point home?

Chapter 1 Key Ideas

- Go beyond telling your stakeholders what they have a right to know; think hard about what you really want them to know.
- Transparency has its risks but has its benefits as well.
- Communication takes time, but taking the time to do it carefully and well is more efficient in the long run and can help you avoid overloading your audiences.

Reflections

- What practices has your district used to tell stakeholders more than the minimum?

Practices Your District Could Use to Tell More than the Minimum

- Hold public meetings to discuss key issues even when they're not required; keep their agendas short and to the point; and provide printed materials audience members can take home.
- Use your communications to describe and explain curricula, and include examples of student work to illustrate your points.
- When preparing communications, ask yourself what you would want to know if you were in your audience's position, then provide that information.

2

SCHOOL DISTRICTS NEED TO ENGENDER TRUST

Schools need the community's trust, and building trust requires communication.

Trust matters because single-handedly we can neither create nor sustain many of the things we care most about.

—Megan Tschannen-Moran[1]

Deborah Meier, a legendary public school reformer in New York City and Boston, notes that trust is both "a goal and a tool."[2] It's a goal because your district couldn't exist if taxpayers didn't trust you with their money and if families didn't trust you with their children. It's a tool because, when your district has earned trust, you can use it to help persuade members of the school community to agree with actions you want to take.

We believe strongly that planned, thoughtful communications play a critical role in winning and retaining trust. Trust is a crucial social dimension in schools, both internally (in relations between leaders and staff members) and externally (between your district and your community).

Anthony Bryk and Barbara Schneider studied school reform in Chicago public schools, focusing on social relationships. They cited studies of school restructuring that concluded that trust and respect are critical to the development of a professional community, and their own research showed that trust "lubricates much of a school's day-to-day functioning and is a critical resource as local leaders embark on ambitious improvement plans."[3]

Stephen R. Covey introduced the concept of the emotional bank account, which he defines as "a metaphor that describes the amount of trust that's been built up in a relationship." He goes on to say, "When the trust account is high, communication is easy, instant, and effective."[4] On the other hand, he argued, a negative balance makes it tough to achieve consensus on difficult issues. Further, Covey contended in a later book, "What about when there's high trust and you make mistakes? They hardly matter. People know you. 'Don't worry about it, I understand.'"[5]

Deposits in your district's trust account grow incrementally—it's a methodical process involving positives such as good test scores, innovative programs, community-supported extracurricular activities, and solid financial practices. Withdrawals come quickly and sometimes unpredictably, resulting from negatives such as poor test scores, a failed tax referendum, bad press, organized political opposition, or an unforeseen crisis.

And the fallout from withdrawals can linger. In our district, previous school leaders reacted to the drop in post–baby boom enrollment by closing and demolishing one of the district's three school buildings during the 1970s. After enrollment bounced back years later, a subsequent board made the difficult decision to build a new building, which opened in 1994. In 2004, when our school district mounted a referendum campaign to raise its property tax rate, we heard from irate community members who still didn't forgive the district for having torn down a treasured school building, only to put a new one in its place. But the district still had enough of an account balance for the referendum to pass by a two-to-one margin.

Researcher Tschannen-Moran also believes people will be forgiving under certain circumstances. She has studied the underpinnings of trust, including benevolence, honesty, and competence. If your constituents believe you have good intentions and their best interests in mind, you can foster trust. If benevolence and caring are viewed as missing, mistrust develops. Your community will forgive failures of execution more easily than failures of intention, Tschannen-Moran wrote. If they think your heart is in the right place, if they believe you're trying to do the right thing, they will eventually forgive your mistakes.[6]

ASSESSING THE LEVEL OF TRUST

Consider how you would answer the following questions about your district:

- Do people disagree with the district's decisions publicly or privately, and how do they make their disagreements known?
- How does the district treat people who disagree?
- Are there groups in your community that do not participate in school events and activities? If so, do you know why not?
- How much do your parents trust their children's teachers?

- How would your teachers characterize trust in the district—between teachers and administrators, board members and teachers, teachers and parents, and teachers and principals?
- How frequently do you hear statements such as "I can't trust him until he proves himself"?

The answers to these questions tell you something about the level of trust within your district. They might also tell you something about how your values, communications styles, and communications practices affect that level of trust. (Querying your audiences about trust and other issues can be done in regular surveys as well as informal conversations. Such questions also might be included in a communications audit, which we discuss in chapter 9.)

High levels of trust can help the district achieve ambitious goals. Some indicators that you're beyond survival mode and have high levels of external trust include

- high levels of satisfaction as evidenced by parent and community surveys, consistently over time;
- extensive parent participation (more than 90 percent) in teacher/student/parent conferences;
- active participation by parents in strategic-plan initiatives and committees (e.g., curriculum, facilities, and finances);
- strong community participation and support for school events; and
- community support for your district's initiatives and referenda.

Markers of high internal trust include

- high levels of satisfaction (as shown by anecdotal reports and surveys) and staff productivity;
- strong involvement of teachers in decisions that affect them (e.g., schedule, budget, curricula, related instructional units, and assessments); and
- a good working relationship with union leadership, focused on improving student learning, with most contract issues or concerns resolved before going through the official grievance procedure.

BUILDING TRUST

Building trust takes years of being open with your financial records and plans (as we suggest in chapter 1). It involves inviting and welcoming outsiders into your decision making—even the most belligerent or negative ones—and giving everyone time to voice their concerns and opinions. It requires defending your well-considered actions without being defensive; cultivating strong relationships among the staff members; taking responsibility and apologizing when you make mistakes; saying "thank you" to your legions of hard workers (paid and volunteer); developing strong parent and community partnerships; and creating and sustaining a school climate conducive to teacher and student learning and emotional well-being. Former superintendent Julia Haley stressed that "people do their very best work if they feel supported. It's so important to recognize them as individuals and let them know how much you appreciate them."[7]

If the level of trust in your district is unsatisfactory, there are good communications practices you can use to improve it. These include creating opportunities for stakeholders to have a voice in the decisions that affect them; communicating openly and honestly; and valuing and acting upon feedback.

Giving Stakeholders a Voice

Your district builds trust when you give stakeholders a voice in planning, implementing, and assessing outcomes. This is not a new concept. W. Edwards Deming, a pioneer in the field of managing workers, was instrumental in helping the Japanese restructure their factories after World War II. William Glasser, an internationally recognized psychiatrist and author, translated and applied Deming's theories to schools. Glasser argued that satisfying basic human needs—survival, love and belonging, power, freedom, and fun—will lead to a quality workplace: "The work environment must be warm and supportive. The workers must trust the managers."[8] In this same vein, to have a quality school, teachers must have a voice and be involved in decisions that affect them.[9]

It's the school leader's business to provide opportunities for stakeholders to have a voice and share their opinions. Some might join your school-improvement or strategic-planning committees, the booster club, or the Parent-Teacher Association (PTA). While not every active parent or community member has the time or drive to become a school board member, many of your board members were probably once active PTA parents. Their successes as volunteers in PTA, the Band Booster Club, or as room parents were stepping-stones to more involvement.

In many districts, parents serve on committees in areas such as facilities, finance, or curriculum. In Schaumburg District 54, a large suburban district of twenty-seven schools and fourteen thousand students outside Chicago, every board committee includes parents. The district's Goals,

Mission, and Vision committee, for example, consists of 25 percent administrators, 25 percent teachers, 25 percent support personnel, and 25 percent parents and community members. Local school leadership teams in each of the twenty-seven schools include at least two parents. Ed Rafferty, the district's superintendent, was honored as Illinois Superintendent of the Year in 2010 for efforts such as these.

Parents and community members can also volunteer in the classroom or library, or teach an after-school enrichment class. Once they're involved, seek their feedback and encourage them to voice their opinions. Move them from *participation* to *engagement*.

Giving parents a voice in the educational decisions that affect their children—asking for their ideas and listening to what they have to say—can also serve as a trust builder. Here's one common example: Often there are parents who ask to meet with the principal because they want their child to be moved to a different classroom. Sometimes, these preferences are related to the classroom assignment of their children's friends, teacher expertise, or problems with another student in the classroom. For many reasons, principals are reluctant to make changes after the school year has begun.

Linda Hanson, search consultant and former principal and superintendent in the northern suburbs of Chicago, would start these discussions by asking parents, "What are you hoping to get out of today's meeting?"[10] For Hanson, these meetings were less about the specifics of a particular issue and more about listening and letting parents be heard—sometimes she made the change, sometimes she didn't. Her ability to listen and use sound judgment outweighed a slavish devotion to consistency and the rule book.

One approach to such a conversation with parents might begin by asking them, "If you had a magic wand, what would you do to change the situation?" Often, parents know what they don't like but aren't sure what they really want. After giving them time to share their views, a school official can offer her or his perspective and one or more options, including what the official thinks would be the best solution.

In one of our schools, the principal would sometimes tell parents the choice was theirs to make. When they heard that they could have the power to decide, they frequently deferred to the principal's solution. Such a gambit is risky, since principals don't want to be seen as ceding authority to parents or failing to support all of their teachers. Yet, most often, the parents and principal made decisions based not on protecting the egos of the teacher or the principal but rather on what was best for the child. By listening and giving parents the power to decide, they could be more open to the recommendations of the principal and staff. Parents felt empowered by the process, and trusting relationships were built.

Being Open and Honest

School leaders need confidence and courage to be open and share information, influence, and control—particularly with their internal audiences. There is good reason to do so. According to Tschannen-Moran, "Fostering open communication can provide a strategic advantage for schools. In schools with a greater level of trust, teachers and other staff members are more likely to disclose more accurate, relevant, and complete data about problems. When communication flows freely, problems can be disclosed, diagnosed, and corrected before they are compounded."[11]

> The test of your district's commitment to openness is this: do you talk about painful mistakes? In October 2007, the U.S. Air Force mishandled the transport of some nuclear-armed missiles. "This was an unacceptable mistake," U.S. Air Force secretary Michael Wynne said at a press conference. "We would really like to ensure it never happens again."[12] At the press conference, Wynne said that, although U.S. military policy is never to discuss deployment of the nation's nuclear arms, he ordered an exception to the policy so the error could be made public. If the Air Force can do it, so can your district.

Most administrators do not have tenure rights and serve at the pleasure of the superintendent or board. Some are not as forthcoming as they could be because they want to please, avoid conflict, or appear to be in control. However, effective leaders are secure enough to let people know that they don't have all the answers.

Dick Streedain, university professor and consultant for the Knowledge Is Power Program (KIPP), was principal of a K–8 school in an affluent Chicago suburb. In 1988, the school was in the national spotlight after a woman from the community entered the building, shot and killed a boy, and wounded five other children. This tragic event had repercussions for the school community for years to follow.

Faculty meetings during the year following the shooting focused mainly on dealing with posttraumatic stress in this small elementary school community. In the second year, the faculty was ready to resume conversations about instruction, and Streedain was surprised by the growth of factions and polarization. When he met with grade-level representatives prior to the faculty meeting, conversations were rich and productive. But in the large group meetings, Streedain could sense that something wasn't right, so he decided to address the issue. "I don't know what we're doing but our faculty meetings aren't working," he told the large group. "Let's spend a few meetings to talk about what a good faculty meeting looks like."[13] Reflecting on the group dynamics later, Streedain attributed much of the dysfunction to the fact that teachers were at varying stages of the grieving process. There were also new staff members who hadn't experienced the trauma, which made it harder for them to feel part of the group that had.[14]

Because he had spent years building relationships and focusing on emotional needs of staff, he was willing to take the risk that his trust bank balance would allow him to confront his faculty about their dysfunctional meetings. His honest and forthright communication resulted in some workable solutions to the problem. The group decided that the rich grade-level conversations should occur with everyone at the regularly scheduled meetings. Meetings would be less frequent but for longer periods of time, to allow for deeper discussions. And, occasionally, secretaries, custodians, and other support staff members would join them. Outside experts would be invited to consult on instructional issues, and Streedain would no longer run the meetings. The agenda would now be determined by the teachers. According to Streedain, he was following the advice of author and consultant Margaret Wheatley: "Goodbye, command and control!"[15]

Streedain's story highlights the power of honesty and frank communication. He and his teachers were able to identify common interests and build a shared vision of a good faculty meeting, and then a strengthened professional learning community. By having his faculty take charge of the agenda, he was not only modeling good communications, but he was also distributing leadership and strengthening the organization. (Contrast Streedain's behavior to that of another superintendent, in a district near ours. When she was hired, the first thing she did when moving into her office was to request that a lock be put on her door. That sent a message to her staff: "I don't trust you.")

Leaders can also gain trust by communicating trust. Superintendent Rafferty facilitates trusting relationships between board members and union representatives through his board communication teams, which began when he became superintendent in 2004 and his board asked for them. The union arranges for each board member to meet regularly with two certified union staff members and one support staff member. Rafferty has nothing to do with the assignments. Board members receive an agenda ahead of time so they can get information from administrators prior to the meeting if they need it. After the meeting, the board member often communicates with other board members and the superintendent to share any new concerns that union members are raising.[16]

The Illinois Education Association, the state teachers' union, likes this practice, but some of Rafferty's fellow superintendents have a hard time with it. "I know that some of my colleagues need to control all communications," he said. "But I'm not like that." It certainly flies in the face of conventional wisdom, which says that interactions between the board and the staff must go through the superintendent—a viewpoint favored by the Illinois Association of School Boards among many others. And it may work better in large districts, where it is much harder for board members to stay well informed, than in small ones. But it works for Rafferty.

Rafferty is not only working to build trust, but he is also distributing the responsibility for communications. Researcher James Spillane might say this would be an example of "distributive leadership."[17] To put it another way, Rafferty is sharing power, and he is not nervous about it at all. "Actually if you give up control you really have more," he said. When a board member has a question, Rafferty tells him or her the right person to call—and that could be a teacher, a support staff person, or someone in his administration. His board members know they don't need his permission to call anyone they want, but they always let him know anyway.

Rafferty is an example of a leader who extends trust, one of the thirteen behaviors of high-trust people that Stephen M. R. Covey describes. "Not only does it [extending trust] build trust, it leverages trust. It creates reciprocity; when you trust people, other people tend to trust you in return. Additionally (and ironically), extending trust is one of the best ways to create trust when it's not there."[18] And Covey speaks directly to leaders' most natural fear: "Don't withhold trust because there is risk involved."[19]

Stacey Childress, a senior lecturer at Harvard Business School, wrote about efforts in Montgomery County, Maryland, to improve student outcomes and close the achievement gap for minority students. One reason the district was successful was the superintendent's determination to alter the traditional roles and responsibilities of the school board, leadership team, principals, teachers, and parents. The superintendent's "willingness to blur the lines rather than consolidate power to himself was a first step."[20] Because Rafferty is willing to blur the lines, extend trust, and open more channels of communication in Schaumburg, Illinois, many stakeholders are actively involved in his district's school-improvement efforts.

> The way our schools are structured, some individuals are in a unique position to influence students and families. Coaches, physical education teachers, music directors, or theater teachers, for example, tend to have multiyear relationships with kids and might be the staff members with whom students are closest. School secretaries and office personnel, who often are the "face" and "voice" of the school to families and outside visitors and who likely live in the community, are frequently named by parents as trusted communicators. Any serious communications effort should take relationships such as these into account, and your district should work to ensure that all staff members understand—and can deliver—your core messages.
>
> When District 73½ mounted a tax-increase campaign in 2004—its first in fourteen years and an effort that passed by a two-to-one margin—teachers and support staff members played a significant role by canvassing and attending coffees after hours. The most successful "coffee team," by far, was a pairing of the district's recently retired band director (a thirty-three-year veteran) and a social studies teacher who had been with the district for more than forty-five years. Saturday-morning canvassing teams included staff members, and district families responded well to visits from current or former teachers. These people had established long-term relationships with parents, students, and community members, and it was critical to the district's long-term future to build upon those relationships. It should be noted that the administrators scheduled communications training for all the volunteers on how to address the voters and respond to their questions and concerns.

Another aspect of demonstrating openness is physical space—opening your facilities. In these days of heightened security concerns, it's perhaps more difficult than ever to create an inviting atmosphere for your families, volunteers, and other visitors. But while safety for students and staff members must always be a primary objective, it's critical not to lose sight of the benefits the district gains by letting the community see what (and how) you're doing.

The more your families and other community members believe they have access to the district and its buildings, the more they think they can trust you. Conversely, when people feel they're in the dark or unwelcome, they lose trust. There are many ways to make visitors welcome in your buildings. Your district could invite parents to sit in on classes on their schedule, rather than yours. Or your district could make space available for civic functions or to community groups. You could even use technology to offer online "virtual tours." The most important question to answer is this: how do people feel when they visit your buildings?

In our district, the middle school principal once had a conversation with a community resident who was hired by the music teacher to tune the school's piano. He stopped her in the hall to say how impressed he was with the students, commenting that they were friendly and helpful—one even held open the front door for him that morning and helped bring in his equipment. He added that he did not observe the same civility and caring in neighboring schools, and said he refers often to "the school where children are really well behaved and nice." Thus did an incidental visitor become a goodwill ambassador for the district.

Valuing and Acting upon Feedback

Asking the right questions and getting good information are key elements to good school communications, but in order to gain trust, your district must be willing to share feedback and act on what is learned. Here's an ironclad communications rule: if you conduct a survey, make sure you report the results quickly and completely.

Furthermore, if you learn that some in your community have serious issues, you can't just expect them to go away. Your district must be willing to respond by seriously considering changes.

It took us a while to learn that lesson in our district. For several years, demand for a program for gifted and talented students had been a hot topic, with some parents very vocal about wanting better services for that particular group of children. Concerns about the lack of gifted education came up in parent comments and surveys repeatedly, perhaps because we failed to respond appropriately before. When we created or modified gifted programs, we didn't adequately evaluate the programs and report the progress (or lack thereof) to the community.

We think we finally got it right in 2008 when we convened a task force and invited concerned parents, board members, teachers, and administrators to gather information and help us design a program. It began in fall 2009 and is our district's best effort yet to address the community's concerns. The rollout was accompanied by a series of community meetings to explain the plan, a detailed article in the community newsletter and website, and a pledge to track and report on the plan's progress.

Similarly, Honeoye Falls–Lima Central School District in New York state relied on improving communications to rebuild trust after the community reacted negatively when the administration leased $235,000 worth of laptop computers for the district's middle schoolers. It wasn't the decision the community objected to—it was the way it was handled. Administrators wrote,

> The community was quiet for much of the fall. Unbeknown to us, people were talking—they just weren't talking to us. They didn't think we'd listen.
>
> Through the years, the community had shared in the district's education planning via their votes at budget time. The district had given voters the power regarding decisions such as allocating $125,000 for an optional extended-day kindergarten program, which they readily approved.
>
> But we didn't follow that inclusive process this time. Community members had little input into the laptop program. A week before the budget vote, several residents asked the board of education to add the laptop project to the ballot, but it was too late. Board policy required that a proposition of this nature be submitted to the board 60 days in advance of the budget vote. Despite explanations by board members, the community members felt like they had been dealt another blow.[21]

When the district's budget passed by a very narrow margin, in contrast to previous years, school officials knew they had a problem. The district formed a community communications committee made up of twelve community members and two administrators. Through that committee, the district learned of issues leaders didn't know existed. They moved quickly to address concerns, change some plans and practices, and collaborate on ways to move the district forward. District leaders concluded,

> We learned through this process that regardless of how busy we are in our daily work, we must take the time to be careful observers and critical listeners. We must stay in tune with what is going on inside and outside the walls of our schools.
>
> Student learning is at the heart of every decision we make, but the success of our education programs depends in great measure on the trust and support we gain from the community through honest, open communication.[22]

Fred Brill, superintendent in Lafayette, California, learned early in his career how important it is to listen.

> On my first day on the job as Area Superintendent in Oakland, I was unloading boxes from my car when I was met by twenty-five Latino parents who were complaining about their principal, who happened to

be Latina. These parents had met with her and they were concerned that she was chewing gum as she was talking to them and that she had rolled her eyes in a dismissive way.

These parents were really looking to be heard, to be listened to, to be acknowledged, which was challenging because I needed to communicate through a translator. Yes, it required a significant investment of my time, not just in that meeting, but ongoing follow-up and expression of concern. It's not about the language you speak. It's really about the concern, caring, and commitment that you're able to convey in your communication, regardless of the stakeholder group you're talking to.[23]

Chapter 2 Key Ideas

- Planned, thoughtful communications play a critical role in winning and retaining trust.
- Assess the level of trust throughout your organization regularly, and think about how to keep deposits flowing into your trust account.
- Give stakeholders a voice in planning, implementing, and assessing outcomes.
- Use every opportunity to reach out to stakeholders.

Reflections

- What practices has your district used to build trust?

Practices Your District Could Use to Build Trust

- Admit your mistakes and explain what you will do to rectify them.
- Get teachers involved in issues that matter to them, such as schedule building or interviewing candidates for teaching or administrative positions.
- Invite parents and other stakeholders to participate on committees and make meetings at times and places that are convenient for them.
- Identify some of your ardent critics and try to involve them in solving the problem they have raised.

3

SCHOOL DISTRICTS NEED TO ADVOCATE FOR THEMSELVES

Through communication, schools make the case for public support.

The community must not only think well of the public schools, but they must also support the schools with their votes, their tax dollars, and their volunteer hours.

—Kitty Porterfield and Meg Carnes[1]

If ever there were a time when communities placidly accepted and politely applauded all the actions of their school districts, that time is not now. School leaders are continually struggling to find the resources they need to do their jobs well; public schools face greater competition than ever, from private schools, charter schools, and homeschooling; and the public's dim view of school leadership grows. Just look at how big-city mayors are taking control of urban school districts,[2] or how federal education officials and business leaders (and many others) say public schools are failing and must be held accountable.[3]

That means that school districts must be their own best advocates—to the public at large and to each of the audiences that make up their school communities (there's more on how those break down in the next chapter). Carefully planned and executed communications help districts with this critical task.

If your district has all the money it needs to provide your students with an outstanding education, we salute you. We suspect that most school leaders don't feel that way, particularly those who endure bruising annual budget battles, make regular trips to lobby state and federal legislators for increased aid, and campaign to pass their budgets or increase their share of tax revenues. Some, such as a group of superintendents in Michigan, have turned to making videos about their districts' financial woes and posting them on school websites.[4]

The interesting thing is, your budget document is a communications tool in itself. It reveals a great deal about the district's goals and priorities to the careful reader (granted, there may not be many of those). As we suggested in chapter 1, your district needs to view its financial reporting not as drudgery but rather as opportunity.

Your district's responsibility to effectively communicate about finances goes hand in hand with its fiduciary responsibility—in fact, the two are equally important. If you cannot persuade your community to support your enterprise, you won't be able to run the district effectively. It's that simple.

And there's some evidence to indicate that—contrary to the impression you might get from conversations with irritated taxpayers—many in the community give school financial issues thoughtful consideration, rather than reacting in knee-jerk fashion. In a 2009 national Kappan Gallup Poll of public attitudes toward public schools, 32 percent of the respondents listed lack of school funding as the number 1 problem facing education today, *the highest percentage ever recorded*.[5] So it seems as though more people than ever are willing to at least listen to your district when it has to make the case for more money.

In this chapter, we will discuss circumstances and situations that require districts to be advocates, and communication strategies and tactics that can help your district advocate for itself.

COMMUNICATING IN A CAMPAIGN

In 2003, our district faced a one-million-dollar deficit (in a total budget of about fourteen million dollars), and after much deliberation the school board made the painful decision to ask the taxpayers to approve the maximum allowable increase in the property tax rate. The last referendum had been in 1990, and in the intervening years the district tried to earn a reputation in the community for being fiscally conservative. In a community where considerably fewer than half of the voters had children enrolled in the public schools, where property tax rates were already the second highest compared to neighboring districts (largely because the commercial and industrial tax base is disproportionately low), we had a daunting task ahead of us.

So how did we advocate, and what communication strategies did we use?

- More than a year before the referendum vote, we began holding meetings to educate our community on our financial situation and give them opportunities to ask questions.
- At our community meetings, we asked attendees whether they would support a tax-increase referendum if necessary, and if so, how? We listed specific tasks (canvassing, fundraising, and organizing outreach) for which people could indicate their interest and asked for contact information to start a database of potential volunteers. For those who indicated they would not support a tax increase, we asked them what further information we could provide that might change their minds.
- A community volunteer who was a communications professional worked with our core committee of volunteers to develop a strong, memorable campaign message (we say more about message development in chapter 5). That message—"Good neighborhood schools are the heart of a strong community"—was repeated throughout the campaign, verbally and on buttons and printed materials.
- We used face-to-face meetings and printed materials to provide community residents with data on staff and administrative salaries, test scores, long-range financial projections, and the cuts that had been made in recent budgets. We created different print materials for different audiences (see chapter 4 for more on differentiation)—some just had bullet points, while others contained detailed questions and answers (see appendix 1 for some examples).
- Informal coffees held in the homes of more than fifty residents gave us a platform for volunteers including parents, teachers, and administrators to talk to—and listen to—neighbors. As we noted in chapter 2, our most successful volunteers were veteran teachers who were known and trusted.
- Some coffees, organized by leaders in our immigrant communities, targeted non-English speakers. We held these meetings in Tagalog, Hindi, Gujarati, Arabic, Assyrian, Spanish, Korean, and Chinese.
- Canvassers went door-to-door in teams of two, frequently pairing a parent or community volunteer with a teacher. For many individuals—no matter how committed to education they may be—the thought of knocking on a stranger's door and making a referendum sales pitch seems impossibly difficult. Having a companion lets each

person share the daunting task, and having a teacher as part of the team increases the chance that someone in the house might know a canvasser. We also tried to make canvassing easier and more efficient by analyzing our lists and concentrating on households that seemed most likely to be receptive.
- We made two commitments: even if the tax increase passed, the district would still cut one hundred thousand dollars from the budget and would do all in its power to push the next referendum as far into the future as possible. After the vote, we made the cuts, and six years later, the district has held to the second promise. (As Stephen R. Covey might say, we made a huge deposit in our trust account by keeping our word.)

COMMUNICATING IN A POLITICALLY SAVVY WAY

Griff Powell served as superintendent in Illinois and New York for twenty-two years in eight school districts, three as an interim superintendent. During his tenure, he was involved in fourteen referenda, twelve of which passed.

One of Powell's tactics was to form a relationship with whoever was in charge of the dominant political organization in the area. Before meeting, he did his research about the politician, and then tried to establish a personal connection—sometimes it was a lively talk about wrestling (Powell had been a coach); sometimes it was a discussion about alma maters. Once a connection was made, Powell would make his case. Often, he knew that it would be unrealistic for the politician to advocate for a tax increase on the school district's behalf. In that case, Powell asked him or her to "please remain neutral."[6] While he might not be able to count on organizational muscle, at least he could defuse opposition.

Another of Powell's tactics was to actively appeal to the majority of the community that did not have children in school. He routinely got involved in community activities outside school and made it his business to live in the district in which he worked. Thus, when he talked about a referendum, he could talk about "raising *our* taxes, not *your* taxes."

In addition to doing volunteer work for Rotary and the Chamber of Commerce, he organized senior citizen "proms." He visited nursing homes and senior citizen residences and urged seniors to vote for the referendum to make the community a better place to live. "I got them registered to vote," he says. "Sometimes people don't vote if they're not asked to."

TURNING CRITICS INTO ADVOCATES

People who contact your district because they have an issue or concern are targets for engagement. You should take advantage of the fact that they have taken the initiative to call you or send you an e-mail. It might seem counterintuitive, but if you can take time to listen and embrace those people who have been complaining, they might end up helping your district.

Julia Haley, a former superintendent in suburban Chicago known for her ability to build relationships, always counseled her principals: "The only thing you can give people is time." When you set up a meeting, even if your time is limited, you should give your visitors sufficient time to make their argument. Don't be like some administrators who, before beginning a meeting, put their watch on the table to restrict the amount of time for the conversation. Try to reach common ground, even if you can't do all someone demands that you do.

Business consultant Susan Lucia Annunzio extols the value of "respectful communication." She writes, "The two most important rules in respectful communication are: Always assume good intent, and identify the logic. If you assume that someone's motives for bringing up a particular idea or making a comment are in the best interests of the company—that they are not driven by an ulterior motive or self-interest—you are much more likely to find out what is smart about the idea. If you assume negative intent, you're likely to label the idea or the person: 'That's a dumb idea,' or 'She's stupid.' But your job is not to label; it's to comprehend."

She goes on to warn, "If you don't practice respectful communication, you are in danger of missing a brilliant idea."[7]

In 2008, National-Louis University professor Linda Tafel attended a board meeting in our district for the first time. She was there to make a presentation about a new university partnership with the district. During the meeting, an angry and frustrated senior citizen complained about his rising tax bill and the construction cost for a new addition.

Tafel was struck by how cordial the board members were. They listened intently to the agitated gentleman and interacted with him, asking him clarifying questions and engaging him. She said she had often seen board members pay little attention and merely wait for speakers to get their comments over with. In this case, she thought the board demonstrated a key attribute of respectful communication—listening.[8]

We learned the value of respectful communication in 2008 when a small group of vocal parents raised concerns about the district's foodservice—specifically about choices students were making and the nutritional value of some of the offerings. Some parents wanted organic foods served and no sweets or desserts. One parent used the Freedom of Information Act (FOIA) to request a copy of the district's contract with its foodservice provider to determine for herself whether the company was making an unreasonable profit by offering low-cost, unhealthy foods.

While this topic was a high priority for the parents, it was a relatively low one for administrators, especially since the superintendent was in her first year and had many strategic-plan initiatives to focus on. Her administrative team asked, "Why do we have to meet with them? We have so many other issues to deal with now!" "And is it really our job to get everybody to eat spinach?"

Nevertheless, the district formed a task force to study the issues. It was clear that the parents needed to learn more about the district's constraints, and school leaders needed to understand the parents' concerns and figure out whether they could improve the foodservice program.

The district had developed a wellness policy in response to federal legislation in 2004.[9] But the parents with complaints wanted the plan to be much more specific, especially as it related to nutrition and foodservice. They argued that the district was not implementing its wellness policy as best as it could.

On the other hand, these parents didn't know the district's financial situation well and didn't understand why the district couldn't allocate the additional twenty thousand dollars they desired. School leaders needed to communicate their position and continue advocating for their conservative approach to spending.

The superintendent and her administrative team took a challenging situation and listened respectfully. They tried to understand the parents' interests and concerns, and made it clear that they were open to change. Parents learned about the district's foodservice goals and the constraints that the district faces. Not all issues could be resolved to every parent's satisfaction, but most parents on the task force felt good about their interactions with the district and were pleased that common interests had been identified and that some solutions were agreed upon.

The district continues to look at ways to increase the nutritional value of the lunches while adhering to government regulations. The parent who made the FOIA request volunteered to write a column for the schools' weekly news, highlighting the nutritional value of food being served that week. She also volunteers in the cafeteria and has joined a committee to review and revise the district's health and wellness plan. School leaders learned that they needed to communicate more effectively about the lunch program while continuously exploring ways to increase the nutritional value of the food offered.

There are three lessons here: your district can always do better; good solutions and recommendations can come from anyone; and since your critics aren't just going to go away, you're better off listening to them.

Two other examples of turning your critics into strong advocates come from Twin Rivers Unified School District in northern Sacramento County, California, which received the 2010 Communications Award from the National School Public Relations Association (NSPRA). Director of Communications Trinette Marquis tells of a parent who criticized some of the writing in the district's publications. This parent is now editing for the district for free. According to Marquis, "She does great work!"[10]

Marquis also discussed a more serious issue, when the district convened a facilities task force—including community members—to make preliminary recommendations about school closings. The task force presented its findings at a series of community forums. At one of the meetings, a parent stood up on a table and told everyone in attendance, "There is a conspiracy here, and they're not sharing all the details with you."[11] He wanted those in the audience to stay and meet with him. Marquis later spoke with him, listened to his concerns, and tried to convince him that the task force and administration really did want to hear what the community had to say and that there was no preordained plan of action.

Following their conversation, he sent Marquis an e-mail: "If ever I can assist you let me know. . . . I know it's 'your job' or whatever but I feel as though I owe you. . . . I'll tell my little herd of followers that the big bad district is capable of listening or responding to the needs of its folks. I may or may not agree with whatever happens when this stuff gets decided, but I have no qualms with the way things have gone down."

He also e-mailed the board, thanking them for getting him engaged, and added,

> The meeting held on Thursday night could NOT have been more different than the one last week. I was truly impressed with the changes in format. I intend to appear at the next Board meeting to speak to this [issue] in person with the same passion I spoke against it at the other meeting. I have not ever taken such a role in my local school, and the

last 10 days or so I have literally centered my life around getting to these various meetings and having my voice heard. I feel encouraged as I have gone through this process, encouraged by a system that allows persons like myself to take a part in something as crucial as our community's children. I believe that by simply taking a part in this whole process, especially in these trying times, has made me a better informed, better involved citizen and parent, and possibly a better person.[12]

As Twin Rivers superintendent Frank Porter notes, "Listening well is a key to success for every superintendent. Parse out what is valuable criticism and use that to guide your actions. People see that you act on what they say when what they're saying has critical viability and truth."[13]

USING THE MEDIA TO HELP YOU ADVOCATE

Bill Berg, a journalist-turned-media consultant, has this to say about talking to the press: "The rationale usually goes as follows: 'Don't tell them [media] anything. It will all blow over. The less said, the better it will be.' There was a time . . . perhaps about thirty or forty years ago . . . when that was probably pretty good advice. Today, it ranks right up there with holding your breath until the paramedics arrive!"[14]

As Berg notes, the days of hunkering down in the face of media coverage are over. It's part of a school leader's job to be the public face and voice of the district. You can do that part of your job well if you take it seriously and plan for media encounters.

When dealing with reporters, remember what Annunzio said about respectful communication—don't assume your questioners have bad intent. As a local reporter in our district argues, you should look at the media as an extension of your community. Although you can't control what stories run or how they're written, and you can't always be sure that you will be quoted accurately, the fact is reporters are trying to tell the community what's going on. That should be your goal, too.

Besides being respectful, be responsive. Return phone calls promptly. Reporters are people, too, and you can improve your relationship with them by helping them meet a tight deadline.

However—and we can't stress this enough—make sure you have your facts straight *before* you pick up the phone. Always take time to prepare what you want to say, so that you don't lose track of your key messages during your conversation. This is equally true for press conferences, face-to-face interviews, or on-camera appearances.

If you think your district has a good story to tell, contact your local media and let them know. Don't wait for them to figure it out. As traditional media outlets face diminishing budgets, reporters' time and attention get stretched. You can help them by pointing out useful stories, and they can help you by getting your stories told.

Superintendent Ed Rafferty, whom we mentioned in chapter 2, writes nine articles a year for the newspaper that covers his area. "I write them. Nobody else," he noted. He doesn't even filter them through his communications person: "It has to be my writing. They're pretty informal and the idea was suggested by the district's Communication Council."[15]

Rafferty's first article of the year focuses on goals and projects, and the last is usually a celebration of the district's successes. He views the articles as an opportunity to thank or acknowledge someone or educate the public on one of the district's initiatives. For example, he wrote one piece explaining why the district's elementary schools don't handle security "lockdowns" the same way the high schools do. Another time, he wrote about what it takes to get the schools open when there's a snowstorm, and one of the district's custodians responded, "I'm glad you know how hard we work!"

Because all district employees don't live in the newspaper's coverage area, Rafferty shares the monthly articles directly with staff. He receives about thirty responses a month from staff members. When he gets an e-mail, he responds within twenty-four hours. He has been surprised by the reaction to his columns, saying, "I didn't think of the impact my articles would have, but it's huge."

School leaders must use every opportunity and every tool at their disposal to advocate for their school or district. We'll leave the last word for Porterfield and Carnes, the communications consultants whom we cited at the beginning of this chapter:

> Superintendents and principals have a lot of persuading to do. Sometimes the job is a big one—like selling a new bell schedule, and sometimes it is just introducing the new third-grade teacher. The concerned audience isn't always parents. Sometimes it's the whole staff, or the teachers, or the city council. Sometimes it's the neighbors. . . . Leading the way into new territory almost always means there is a lot of persuading to do.[16]

Chapter 3 Key Ideas

- School districts must advocate for themselves to the public at large and to each audience.

- Explain how you prioritize the district's goals and initiatives and allocate resources to achieve them.
- Practice respectful communication and assume good intent on the part of your critics.
- Remember that your district can always do better, and good ideas can come from anyone.
- Your critics are not going to just go away; you're better off listening to them.
- Be proactive when you have a good story to tell.

Reflections

- What practices has your district used to advocate?

Practices Your District Could Use to Advocate

- Make your case at community meetings—even when they're not required—on school finances, new curriculum, new programs, and other key issues.
- Join with leaders from neighboring districts to meet with elected representatives and community leaders to discuss education legislation and key issues.
- Develop relationships with the reporters who cover your district; tip them in advance on upcoming issues and events; make sure they know how to contact you for further information; prepare to be interviewed; and take their calls.
- Use committees and task forces to get stakeholders involved; take advantage of opportunities to ask people to volunteer; keep a running list of people you encounter who might make good participants.

Part II

HOW BEST TO COMMUNICATE

4

KNOW WHO'S LISTENING AND HOW TO REACH THEM

Schools must understand their audiences and their means of communication.

To enlist people in a vision, leaders must know their constituents and speak their language. People must believe that leaders understand their needs and have their interests at heart. Leadership is a dialogue, not a monologue. To enlist support, leaders must have intimate knowledge of people's dreams, hopes, aspirations, visions, and values.

—Jim Kouzes and Barry Posner[1]

Just as your teachers differentiate instruction to ensure that it is appropriate for each student, so must your district differentiate its communications. You need to consider all of your audiences—students, parents, teachers, board members, and other members of the community. That includes understanding each audience's different role in the school community and each audience's different need for and access to information. In addition, you must understand the advantages and disadvantages of each potential method of communication.

With respect to differentiating among internal audiences, you already know that students, teachers, and parents need different information at different times. Here's how education experts and authors Richard Stiggins, Judith Arter, Jan Chappuis, and Steve Chappuis put it:

> The level of detail needed depends on the decision to be made. Teachers and students need detail about specific standards and enabling learning targets because they are making specific decisions about what has been learned and what should come next. Parents need highly descriptive

information at times, especially when we request their intervention. At other times they need to know only that learning is progressing on track. This is true of others as well. For example, instructional support personnel may need very detailed information, while administrators may require general summaries of student achievement to meet their decision needs.[2]

With respect to external audiences, the communications plan for Boston Public Schools states, "Some forms of communication may be appropriate for reaching all of these target audiences, but more often, the messages and means of conveying information should be tailored to each group to address its particular needs."[3]

The key questions are, do you give careful thought to what information flows to each different audience and how it gets there? If you do, then you're already thinking *strategically* about your communications. If you don't, you're certainly not alone—and this chapter is meant to help you think in a different way than you have in the past.

KNOW YOUR AUDIENCES

For purposes of deciding what to say and how to say it, organizations generally divide audiences for their marketing communications into two camps: internal (i.e., employees) and external (i.e., customers and the public at large). Most school communications plans do the same thing, and for the most part, the divide works reasonably well. Take a look at table 4.1 for a breakdown.

There is not universal agreement on how students and their families should be treated in such a scheme; some districts say parents are an internal

Table 4.1. Breakdown of Internal and External Audiences

Internal Audiences	External Audiences
Students	Alumni and their families
Parents of students in your district	Families without students in your district (i.e., private school families and homeschool families)
Administrators	
Teachers	
Support staff	Community residents with no children
School board	Local business operators
	Community leaders (i.e., elected officials, religious leaders, and heads of civic organizations)
	News media
	Communities beyond district borders

audience, some say external. Some don't list students at all; some even list students as internal and parents as external.

Rather than agonize over how to divide your audiences, it's likely more productive to understand that, while some of your audiences are internal and some are external, your internal audiences must get the same information and messages your external ones do, with more besides. For example, the Alum Rock (California) United Elementary District lists as a standing element of its communications plan, "Distribute all external publications and news releases to employees via Email, and post on website."[4] In other words, make sure your employees know what the rest of the community knows.

Internal audiences are close to the action—they work for or with you, and from experience they know a lot about the daily life of your schools and how your district goes about its business. Let's look more closely at each group and the communications they need to receive.

Students get a lot of communication from your district—ranging from the mundane details of the daily schedule to their report cards and other things that describe how well they're doing. Besides these, it is important that the district communicate to students what they are expected to learn, how they are expected to progress, and the attitudes and behaviors they are expected to display. The district must also convey its regard for students' well-being. All of this information needs to be communicated at a level of detail most external audiences don't need.

Parents also receive a high volume of communication from your district, relating mostly to the same things that student communications cover. In addition, you must communicate with them about ways they can contribute to their children's education and keep them informed about the events and activities that make up school life. Beyond that, you must at times communicate with parents as members of the larger community, telling them about district finances, facilities, curriculum, and goals—all the things that have to do with your district but that are not specifically about their children.

Administrators require the most detail of any audience. Someone (or everyone) in the administrative team or cabinet needs access to the details about everything that internal and external audiences may have questions about. They are the ones who ensure effective communications with all groups. They need to communicate well with each other to do that.

Teachers need four kinds of communication: information about their employment (compensation and benefits, workplace policies), information that makes them better teachers (curriculum and professional development), information about their students (test results, previous teachers' experiences, family issues), and information about the school and district (as discussed above for parents). It's sometimes easy for districts to focus on the first three and forget the fourth, but they are all critical.

Support staff members need the same employment and district information as do teachers. Again, it's important to remember that employees need to know how the district is doing and what it intends to achieve. Unless they know what you're trying to accomplish, they can't help you. The plan in Twin Rivers notes, "One of our primary objectives is to ensure that our employees understand key objectives, strategies, and messaging so that we maintain consistency and accuracy in our interactions with outside audiences."[5] This is true for administrators and teachers as well.

Your school board is a unique audience—internal because of board members' responsibility to manage the district, external because they represent the larger community. They need to know something about everything that affects students, parents, and staff members, although generally not in as much detail as each affected group does. Conversely, they need more detail about the district's overall situation than any other external group does, in order to make the best decisions. They may receive the district's community newsletter at home, but that's not the best way to give them information. If you're doing your job well, they've already gotten all that information—and much more—from board packets, presentations, and face-to-face meetings.

Most of the information internal audiences receive helps them fulfill their roles within the district—the messages are necessary for the district to function day to day. The information external audiences receive, on the other hand, tells the story of how the district works and what it's accom-

---

Veteran superintendent Griff Powell placed great emphasis on communicating with his board members. He talked with them on a regular basis and would take responsibility when things went badly. "You can't easily blame seven people but you can blame one," he said. "[Accepting blame] was my job." He also believed it was critical to give all the board members the same information. So when he spoke first to the board president, he would end the conversation by saying, "I now need to inform the other board members. Do you want to tell them or do you want me to?"[6]

plishing. Those messages are needed to influence how the district is viewed by the community and to gain support.

Alumni and their families have a connection with your district and are likely more interested in knowing what the district is doing than are families without students in your district or residents with no children. For the alums, some direct communication is worthwhile to reinforce their connection. But members of all these groups live in your district, pay taxes, and vote. Consistent, informative communication (through periodic mailings, local access cable TV, or online, for example) provides all of them with reasons to support your district.

Local businesses also pay taxes, and many of their employees live in your district and vote. Your communication needs to show that you understand their concerns, and it needs to address ways your district provides valuable service to them. The examples cited above can help do that; the kind of Rotary or chamber of commerce involvement that former superintendent Griff Powell practiced (see chapter 3) helps in this area as well.

Community leaders are crucial to shaping the perception of your district in the larger community. Because they influence the opinions of others, you have to communicate with them effectively and build positive relationships with them. You want to be sure they have the knowledge and information needed to support your initiatives and counter misinformation when it occurs. Involvement in civic or religious organizations is a way of putting yourself in a position to communicate your key messages to these leaders.

Members of the news media are a small but vital audience because the stories they write and produce can strongly influence the opinions of others—many others, depending on their circulation or ratings. Your district needs to provide them with materials that are exceptionally clear and detailed, to minimize the chance of misunderstanding. Just as important, you need to cultivate relationships with local reporters who can help your district convey its messages accurately when issues are complex or controversial.

Those who live in communities outside your district don't directly affect your success or failure. But they may have an opinion about your district, owing to media coverage or history. Your district's reputation is important particularly when young families are deciding where to live, or when neighboring districts are competing for scarce state and federal resources. For example, the Elmira (New York) City School District specifically identifies local real estate agents as an audience to be addressed because of the district's intent to woo families of young children.[7] It's worth devoting some resources to communication that enhances your district's image.

A Special Case of Differentiation

More and more, districts find that they need to communicate to non-English-speaking families. Translation thus becomes another kind of differentiation—one that's a little tricky to accomplish in an organized manner.

Your central office or your district's English Language Learners (ELL) teachers may have provided translated information to students and families for a long time, and it's quite common for bilingual students to translate for their families. But it's a long way from ad hoc translation to planned communications.

How can your district get a better handle on this? Some recruit volunteers to translate for families. Remember that if your district can assemble a corps of volunteers, you can use them to deliver key district messages, in addition to word of their children's progress and other basic information. Our district began a new program for kindergarten families in 2009 called "Language Ambassadors"; the ambassadors translate for parents who speak the same language. Officials hope these parent volunteer ambassadors will remain involved at least as long as their children are in school and will thus spread the program through all grades eventually.

Districts are also turning to software-driven translations for their websites, which have the advantage of being automated and relatively inexpensive. However, our experience with this jibes with that of a *Wall Street Journal* reporter—the translations can be clumsy and imprecise.[8] As the software gets better, so will this option.

The Peel District School Board, whose 225 schools serve about 150,000 students in three municipalities near Toronto, Canada, took an aggressive and award-winning approach to translation. The district is the second-largest in the country, and 47 percent of its students speak a language other than English at home. In 2006, the district created twenty-five Web "microsites," each fully translated into a different language and linked from its main website, www.peelschools.org.[9] The effort, partly funded by a grant from the Ontario provincial government to help promote parent involvement in the schools, used professional translators to create the content. The plan was executed so well that the district received a Gold Quill Award in 2007 from the International Association of Business Communicators.[10]

The district has also implemented other strategies to engage its newcomers, including multilingual posters at every school, on-the-spot interpreters, settlement workers employed in the schools, and interpreters available for meetings with teachers.

Another option to consider is to take the informal translating that students do for their families a step further. How about having ELL students work with their teachers to prepare short, translated podcasts containing key information such as procedures for reporting absences or signing up for teacher conferences? Podcasts are cheap, are easy to store and access, and can be filed and used for years.

UNDERSTAND YOUR CHANNELS

Your administrators, teachers, support staff members, and board members are all internal audiences—but they don't all get the same information, and you would not communicate with them in the exact same way. The same is true for all of your audiences, internal and external. Part of your task is to know the differences between them, have a good sense of what they need to know, and have some reliable gauge for what communication channels work best for them.

Based on your experience and knowledge of your community, you already have a sense of what information your parents need. But do you know how many prefer getting newsletters in the mail, rather than online? What percentage of your parents, staff members, or the larger community expects to hear from you on the Web, via e-mail, or via Twitter?

Your experience alone won't give your district the knowledge it needs. Good communications planning calls for research to find out from your audiences what they want to know and how they'd like to receive information. If you didn't take marketing in college, the federal government offers a remarkably quick overview of the types of research that can be done, including thumbnail summaries of customer satisfaction surveys, focus groups, search data, and more.[11]

Your district needs to assess its audiences frequently because, as they change (get older or younger, speak different languages, or bring new or different expectations of what schools should be doing), their wants and needs change also. To communicate well, your district must respond appropriately.

Just as you must understand different audiences, you must also understand the characteristics of different means of communication, or channels. Each has its own strengths and weaknesses. Print communications (letters, memos, and newsletters) are what Yale University professor emeritus Edward Tufte calls "high-resolution"; they carry a lot of information in a relatively compact manner.[12] Video or audio communications, by contrast, are lower resolution; they are limited by the number of words and images that can be transmitted and understood per minute. That's why, when a five-hundred-page novel is made into a two-hour movie, three hundred fifty or so pages of plot never make it into the screenplay. E-mails or other electronic short messages carry even less information; they're mostly good for letting your audience know that you have something to tell them, the specifics of which they can learn elsewhere. Many school districts are finding that e-mail "blasts" to their school community can generate substantial interest.[13] Finally, the Web is a combination of all the other media discussed above; it can transmit headlines and short bursts of information, while also having the capacity to present detailed documents. For example, many school districts post all board reports—not just the executive summaries—at their websites.

It's important to remember that each of your channels can work in concert with the others to promote all your messages in all their forms. You'll want to avoid the common mistake of framing your communications in terms of the channels you want to use, rather than the messages you need to convey and the audiences you need to reach. Look at it this way: you wouldn't pick up a pen and think, "There's got to be a way for us to use this to communicate." Each channel is simply a tool, just as pen, paper, or photocopiers are. Here's a closer look at channels and what they can do.

Print communications (letters, fliers, memos, newsletters, and reports) have many advantages: they can carry lots of detail, as Tufte notes; people are used to reading the printed page, no matter what their age or experience; there are systems in place (i.e., the U.S. Postal Service, employee drop boxes, and student backpacks) to distribute them; they are somewhat flexible (you can produce one-page fliers, long reports, or anything in between); your district can control what it says in print; and materials can reach a lot of people. However, printed pieces cost time and money to produce, generate waste (which we hope your district is recycling), can be inefficient (see the box about backpacks elsewhere in this chapter), and aren't as easily updated as a Web page. Your district should use print when you have detail to convey, while being mindful of how much detail a given audience needs. For example, a task force of community members studying your finances needs full reports with lots of information; residents who attend a public forum on your finances should get a brief summary.

Building-based communications (signs, banners, electronic message boards, and video displays) are not meant to transmit much detail. They're good for publicizing activities and events, particularly if you have a system in place for deleting outdated information promptly. They're also good for transmitting short messages that bear repeating, such as your district's slogan or tagline. Tailor those messages to those who have access to the displays. Signs inside the building should address students and staff members, while those on the outside speak to the entire community.

Interpersonal communications (by administrators, teachers, support staff members, board members, students, and parents) are extraordinarily important. The strengths of one-on-one communications are in their credibility (getting information directly from the source) and flexibility (receiving specific answers to specific questions). But your district will get the full value of these communications from staff only through planning and training. As the Twin Rivers (California) "Communications Plan" notes,

> Our employees, specifically those who touch the public most, should feel confident in our understanding of organizational direction so that we can deliver consistent messages. Classified staff, Board of Trustee members, administration, volunteers, and teachers alike are the face and voice of our district. As such, our interactions, our demeanor, our professionalism, and expressed viewpoints all are important pieces of what our "public" thinks about Twin Rivers [Unified School District].[14]

There are costs involved in developing those consistent messages and training staff members to convey them—but given their value, it's time and money well spent.

Interpersonal communications in your district go beyond your staff members. What students, families, and others say about you can be powerful, as the Twin Rivers plan recognizes: "In most cases, the informal communication taking place within our stakeholder communities is just as important as the messages sent in press releases or official speeches."[15] It's important to bring your messages to your external audiences, so that they can repeat them and spread the word even more widely.

Automated telephone calls or phone trees can have impact, if used wisely. Telephone calls, either automated or from a person, can carry valuable short messages (e.g., schools closing during a snow emergency or notice of an important meeting). But if phone calls—especially automated ones—are overused, they lose their effectiveness. They are also limited to those whose phone number you already have, so they likely don't go beyond the families of your students. Also, extreme weather conditions could affect telephone service, and phone trees can break down if not enough people cooperate. Nevertheless, these tools can be useful, and phone trees get some members of your community directly involved with you—a worthwhile side benefit.

News media are always a key component of any district's communications, for three main reasons: their relatively low cost to the district, their ability to reach a large potential audience, and the credibility that stems from their independence. These advantages are undeniable but a little deceptive, because the district can't control the message, and there's no guarantee that community members will read, hear, or view the story. Your district may find that an inaccurate or incomplete published story is worse than no story at all, or that when a positive story appears, too few people see it. All you can do in the first instance is seek a rebuttal or clarification and recognize that not as many people will see it as those who saw the original story. In the second instance, you might photocopy and distribute the story, link to it from your district website, and promote it through other channels you control. In getting your messages out, your district cannot ignore news media, nor can it rely solely upon them.

Student-generated audio and video broadcasts (e.g., local access cable telecasts and school radio stations) offer you the prospect of presenting detailed, engaging information with a lot of control. But their effectiveness relies on the quality of the content and your district's ability to make audiences aware of what's available. Parents love the opportunity to see their children create or perform. To go beyond that—to show the larger community what your students are doing and make a convincing case that their talents are being nurtured and their achievements are significant—means you have to lead them through the clutter of channels to find your broadcasts. Your district can use your other channels (such as print materials, website, and signs) to promote this effort.

Websites have emerged as the communications hub for many districts, because of their manageable cost, ability to reach potential audiences, and flexibility to present short messages or long ones. Because of its ability to deliver audio and video content as well as printed words, the Web also addresses those with varying learning styles. Even with those advantages, your district won't get the maximum benefit from Web communications unless you are able to let people know what's available (as with broadcasting) and keep material fresh and up to date (as with signs).

In 2009, our district adopted a strategy used by many others and redesigned its website with an eye toward directing specific audiences to the content most relevant to them. The basic structure uses a central entry page, with links to audience-oriented "microsites"—including current parents, prospective parents, staff members, alumni, volunteers, seniors, local businesses, and job seekers (see figure 4.1 for an example from Beaverton, Oregon[16]). Users can approach the site by looking for the information they want and can also browse other public areas as they wish.

Figure 4.1. Like many others, the Beaverton, Oregon, school district's home page includes tabs for students, staff members, parents, and the community.

Like websites, e-mail is being used more and more for school communications. Its strength is delivering short messages, and it should be used for emergency notices, to promote events and activities, and to help drive audiences to your district's Web operation. Your efforts to communicate depend on your ability to gather e-mail addresses, so that has to play a role in your e-mail strategy. Another limitation is simply the extent to which your audiences have access to and use the Internet, which also limits the effectiveness of your Web and social media efforts.

Social media (text messaging, Twitter, social networking sites, blogs, and podcasts) are growing rapidly as a way to reach school audiences. Like e-mail, they can be very effective in delivering short messages or driving Web traffic; they too are limited not only by Internet access but also by the fact that some of your audiences don't actively use these tools—at least not yet. However, they hold particular potential (with some attendant problems) for reaching students and recent alumni. There is much more about social media tools in chapter 8.

Suppose your goal is to gain support for a new reading curriculum. Clearly, you want students, parents, and families to know about what's now being taught, how it's different from before, and why you believe the new plan is better. To inform families, you might send printed information home, prepare handouts to distribute at open houses and other school events, post information on your website, hold informational meetings, and publish articles in your newsletter to describe the new curriculum and its benefits. All this information should be geared to a lay audience, meaning it should be written in plain language, jargon free.

You want to make sure teachers and administrators are fully aware of the changes, too, since they're the ones directly responsible for carrying them out. So you send memos, hold meetings, and post information for them as well. This information would be geared to education professionals and should be much more detailed than what you're providing to families.

Don't stop there. By making a significant change to the teaching and learning practices in your district, you've set out to meet a challenge—but you've also created an opportunity to talk to a wider audience about what your district does and how and why it does it. You can start a conversation, and that conversation gives your district a chance to deliver an important message to the entire community—that it works thoughtfully and carefully to address the educational needs of today's children and is diligently building a better future for them.

If your district can deliver that message to alumni and their families, residents who don't have children in your schools, local businesses, and even neighboring communities, it benefits you in ways that go well beyond getting students, parents, and teachers comfortable with a new way of doing things. Explaining a change such as this to the broader community helps you build trust and consensus.

How do you communicate your new program to a broader audience? Use your public channels—community newsletter, local access television, website, public signs, and school building displays. Try to get local news coverage. Invite members of the public into your buildings to show them what you're doing. Do a presentation before a local business group or community organization. Send information to your local elected officials—or better yet, go talk to them. Let them know how you're using the tax money that's allocated to your district.

What do you communicate? Highlight the main points—what you're doing, why you're doing it, and what's changing. Explain the problem your new curriculum is intended to solve. Explain why you think it will work, how your student body has changed, or how new technology fosters new teaching and learning opportunities. Most importantly, explain how the community will benefit from a change that results in more capable young people.

Keep your information short and focused, but have more details ready (on your website, for example) for those who request them. Members of your audience will have differing levels of interest in (or tolerance for) specifics; some will want only the "bottom line," while others want to know more. You can use the varying communication tools at your disposal to satisfy the majority of their needs.

Remember that channels must be used thoughtfully. E-mails, short electronic messages, and headlines on the home page can be used to alert the community to informational meetings on the new reading curriculum but shouldn't be expected to carry any of the background details. Those can go into the newsletter, the letters home, and on a page deeper into the website. Those who want to know how the decision came about, or what other districts' experiences have been with the same curriculum, can probe the PDFs and Web links that reside even deeper in the website (but are linked from the district or curriculum home page). The district can really drive home the point about how necessary and beneficial the change is by posting short audio and video files of teachers and students putting the curriculum into practice. And as time goes on, the district can report on its progress in print, Web documents, and audio and video files as well.

In appendix 2, there's an example of differentiated communications from our district. As part of the district's effort to create a professional learning community, administrators and staff members crafted a set of "power standards" outlining teaching and learning expectations for each grade in each subject area. The documents in the appendix contrast the detailed matrix of the teacher version of literacy standards for second grade with the version of the same standards for parents.

Your district is made up of audiences that are defined largely by how involved they are with the district's day-to-day activities. Their interests may differ to a degree, but they all benefit when your district succeeds—academically, financially, and in myriad other ways. Your district needs to use its communications to keep all its audiences abreast of critical developments, seek their input and participation, and above all, remind them of their stake in your continued success.

Chapter 4 Key Ideas

- Figure out what your district wants to say.
- Effective school leaders tailor or differentiate their communications based on what they know about their different audiences.

- Focus on the message and audience first, and let those determine the communication channels you want to use—the Web, phone blasts, printed newsletters, and so forth.

Reflections

- What practices has your district used to differentiate its communications and take best advantage of its different channels?

Practices Your District Could Use to Differentiate Your Messages and Effectively Use Your Channels

- Survey your audiences frequently to find out what kind of information they'd like to receive and how they'd like to receive it.
- Tailor your information pieces based on what you know your audiences need—highlights and key facts for the general public, more details for affected parents, and even deeper details for teachers.
- Make it easy for stakeholders to communicate with the district—for example, establish a blog on your district's Web page, create regular times when administrators are available to answer questions or hear comments, or maintain a paper or virtual "suggestion box."

5

ALIGN COMMUNICATIONS WITH DISTRICT GOALS AND VALUES

Good school communications flow from district goals and values—and exemplify them.

The strategic leader depends upon principles and values, since they create context for every leadership decision within the system.

—Douglas Reeves[1]

To be effective, your communications need to be aligned with your district's values and goals. By alignment, we mean two things. First, the district's goals and values are described and explained in your communications. The goals and values provide content and context. For example, when your communications address student achievement, they don't just report test scores; they state what the goals are, note whether they are being met, and if not, explain what you're going to do to improve.

Or take this example: The Chicago public school system uses after-school programs to help achieve its goal of raising student achievement. An article that discussed why more teens don't participate in such programs quoted an eighth grader as saying, "[After-school programs] should have some meetings in school, during the school day. Put it in the news. Take pictures of what we do."[2] She's wisely advising the district to make its program—and thus its goal—the subject of its communications.

Second, your communications practices reflect your district's goals and values. If your district prizes openness and honesty, your communications must reflect that. If your district values inclusiveness, you must try to reach as many different segments of the community as possible. Your district's communication practices must be in line with your values.

To put it another way, you have to practice what you preach. Have you witnessed school leaders extol collaboration while hoarding control, praise flexibility while being rigid, or urge civility and respect while being dismissive of parents or staff members? If the values your district posts on the wall aren't evidenced by your actions, it's difficult to argue that they really are your district's values.

With those concepts of alignment in mind, in this chapter we will discuss how to identify and articulate your district's values and how to align those values with your communications practices. At the end of the chapter, we'll take a look at an oft-stated value (giving stakeholders a voice) and see how to align communications practices with it.

IDENTIFYING AND ARTICULATING YOUR GOALS AND VALUES

It's common practice for school leaders to meet with stakeholders (both internal and external) to help articulate the district's values. Such processes are used to design vision and mission statements, strategic plans, or other statements that reflect values and goals. But creating these statements is only the beginning. If they are really going to guide the way you do things in the district, statements can't just gather dust; they must "live off the wall"— translate into action beyond mere words.

Vision Building the First Time Around

In 2003, our district hired a consultant who helped craft a mission statement to make clear our goals and objectives. It was accompanied by a list of beliefs and vision statements for teaching and learning, school culture, and student expectations. About a hundred parents, community members, students, business leaders, teachers, and board members met to help create these statements. In an all-day, facilitated meeting, participants shared their expectations, values, and vision. The process was repeated with the entire teaching and support staff, and a subcommittee meshed the responses from both groups and came up with the statements.

However, in retrospect, what we produced was too long and involved (see appendix 3). No one, except perhaps the superintendent and the consultant, was able to internalize all the messages, let alone make the beliefs come alive or communicate them well.

Vision Building the Second Time Around

Our district tried again in 2008, using an initial group that included parents, administrators, teachers, and members of the community (including some of the same participants from 2003). Two things were different—the process was specifically intended to mesh with the district's new initiative to create a professional learning community (PLC), and drawing on the lesson of the earlier effort, the superintendent was seeking a statement or set of statements short enough to use in the district's day-to-day life.

The process, which again included an all-day brainstorming session facilitated by a consultant, followed by winnowing sessions with representatives of the larger group, resulted in four guiding principles for the PLC. They are as follows:

- Our schools will support and inspire our students.
- Our students will be critical thinkers and creative problem solvers.
- Our community will demonstrate integrity and respect.
- Our graduates will help make the world a better place.

The process also yielded a tagline—"Building a foundation for learning, leadership, and life." The district has integrated the tagline into its communications, including stationery, forms, website, and newsletter, among other vehicles, using a new logo designed by a district parent (figure 5.1 shows the old logo, figure 5.2 the new one).

Figure 5.1. Old logo.   **Figure 5.2. New logo.**

While the values expressed during the two processes were consistent (see appendix 3), they had very different impacts. The second time around, our district made it a priority to create a set of messages that could be easily communicated. We have begun to incorporate the values into district planning and goal setting, and are working to display them in the district's daily activities. For example, we have begun a series of trainings for teachers on how to improve communication with parents and are encouraging them to articulate the guiding principles in their own words in their interactions with families.

USING GOALS AND VALUES IN DISTRICT COMMUNICATIONS

The daily stewards of district goals and values are your administrators and board—the school leaders. These leaders sort through the input from the district's audiences, apply education best practices, direct the effort to achieve the goals, align the district's decisions and processes accordingly, and make midcourse adjustments as necessary. As part of their charge, they must ensure that stakeholders know what the goals and values are. Let's look at communications practices that address that task.

Develop and Deliver Strong Messages

In the field of marketing communications, message development generally involves putting an organization's key people in a room with a facilitator who works with them to draft a short sentence or talking points expressing what an organization most wants its audiences to know. The intent is for the message to be easily remembered and repeated, thus becoming part of the organization's "brand," or identity.

Developing a key message or messages for your district is an important initial step toward communicating with your stakeholders. It can succinctly describe your district's overall mission (or guiding principles, as in our district's example), or it could be designed to support a specific campaign (such as our district's referendum effort, discussed in chapter 3) or program (such as a major change in curriculum, transportation, or facilities).

Concerned about how our financial management was being perceived in the community, in 2006 our district's board and administration held a half-day session to develop a short message to describe how the district goes about its business. Helped by a facilitator, the group came up with this statement: "We believe that if we work together as a team and manage our resources carefully, we can meet the high expectations of our diverse community and ensure the success of each student." The message was used by board members in conversations with community members and by administrators in meetings and media interviews.

Many districts employ the notion of a pithy, repeatable statement or slogan in communicating with students. When our district implemented the Positive Behavior Intervention System (PBIS) ten years ago, we used the tagline "Be responsible, be respectful, and be ready" in written materials and signs, to familiarize students with the program's principles. Classroom teachers and administrators reinforced the message.

Regardless of the purpose, a message works for your district only if you disseminate it many times, through many channels. Most of those channels are obvious—in your district's written communications, on its website, through signs and posters, or on local public-access TV. You can also encourage school leaders to pass the message along when talking with the media, in meetings, and in individual conversations. In communications, this is known as the "elevator speech"—a statement used to get the main point across in the time it takes to go up or down in the elevator.

Furthermore, a message only really works if there's consensus among leaders that it is the right message (a reason the process may need to be facilitated and your district should be sure that all the necessary players are in the room) and that it is used consistently and accurately. In order to ensure this, you might want to draft talking points or answers to frequently asked questions that administrators, staff members, and board members can employ. However, everyone doesn't have to memorize the elevator speech or talking points; people can use their own words, but they have to understand the main concept and be able to get it across.

As noted in chapter 4, you should tailor your message to each audience that will receive it. In promoting a new literacy initiative, for example, your district might emphasize to parents and families that "better readers do better in all academic subjects," while pointing out to local businesspeople that "better readers make better potential employees" and noting to the community as a whole that "better readers make better citizens."

Special Messengers

As we noted in chapter 2, teachers are among the most trusted people in your school community, and you should not overlook their crucial role in shaping the perceptions of your district and building relationships with families. In this excerpt from his book *The Parents We Mean to Be*, Richard Weissbourd—a child and family psychologist at Harvard's Kennedy School of Government and School of Education—provides a particularly clear view of the communicating power teachers wield, knowingly or not:

> It is the spring of my son's sophomore year in high school, and my wife and I find ourselves hustling from classroom to classroom for our parent-teacher conferences, trying to protect our allotted fifteen minutes with each of his five teachers. With three children, we are veterans of this dance, but this evening I find myself battling desolation. It's not that my son is struggling in school or suffering a serious problem; it's that the two teachers we have met thus far have taken us through roughly the same dreary ritual. The teacher begins the session by pulling out a sheet of paper. She recites my son's test scores or grades, and then makes a comment about his being distracted at times and not listening. That "not listening" hangs in the air. I find myself bristling. Is it a euphemism of some kind? Does she find my child difficult? She then reassures us that he is a "good kid."
>
> I don't sense that either of these teachers truly knows my son or cares about what my wife and I are hoping for and fretting about or what we think will help him learn. I know that he does not like one of these teachers and that in his opinion one of these classes is "hell." Yet neither teacher seems to have a clue about his experience.
>
> Then we meet with a third teacher. She starts off the session by telling us how much she enjoys having our son in her class. She describes his willingness to risk being "dumb" by asking questions for the whole class, taking one for the team. She tells us when and how he is confident and when and how he is tentative. She describes his easy relationships with a wide range of classmates and his desire to be helpful. She also talks about his being distracted at times. Yet one of her explanations for this behavior—that any kind of repetitive task is hard for him—helps me understand something about my son that has been opaque to me. She tells us that he never interrupts her or is rude. She asks us how we think he is doing and if we have any concerns, and she listens carefully to our thoughts. I feel that we are in a common project together, a project that is academic but also moral—the project of raising a whole person and a good person. I have to resist the temptation to envelop her in a bear hug.[3]

With some planning, your district can enlist teachers in your efforts to get your key messages across. For example, teachers should be encouraged to discuss your district's goals with parents and families. This requires making sure they know what the goals are and allowing time to cover them in parent-teacher conferences and other contacts. The district should also provide support materials such as brochures or handouts that staff members can refer to and can hand to interested parties. In Edmonds, Washington, district officials recognize the critical role their employees play. "Employees are school ambassadors whose words and actions can either build support from, or destroy the confidence of, a community. Every employee in Edmonds learns that he or she has a responsibility to know what's going on."[4]

In looking specifically at conferences as communication opportunities, you should consider whether your district gives teachers the kind of support they need. Do you assume that every teacher knows how to conduct conferences? What kind of training or advice do you offer? Do you match up new teachers with experienced mentors who can show them the ropes? If so, are you confident that those mentors do a good job with their own conferences? If you don't like the answers to these questions, your district might consider some professional development activities to help teachers improve this critical function. (Our district conducted its first training for all teachers about formal and informal interactions with parents in 2010. See appendix 4 for an outline of that training.)

Use Clear Methods to Report Progress

It's not enough for your district to set goals and align decisions, actions, and resources to them; it must also define how it will measure progress toward achieving those goals. If your district has a good handle on what those measurements ought to be, it has ready-made content for its communications to stakeholders.

It's become common practice to borrow a tactic from corporate strategic planning: the notion of a "balanced scorecard" or grouping indicators that an organization uses consistently to evaluate itself. Beverly Hall, superintendent of Atlanta Public Schools and recipient of the 2009 National Superintendent of the Year award, stated, "The balanced scorecard is our way to look across all departments and ensure they are aligned to our strategy. It gives us transparency and clarity into how our central office (often the target of unfair attacks about a 'bloated bureaucracy') supports the district's progress and children."[5]

Atlanta's deputy superintendent of curriculum and instruction added, "The balanced scorecard forced each and every department to answer the critical question: How does my work support the kids?" Using the balanced scorecard approach facilitated communication throughout this large, central-office system.[6]

For many school districts (and other organizations), the balanced scorecard has translated into a "dashboard" metaphor—an array of measures that give leaders a quick read on how things are going. These indicators are carefully considered and yield valuable insights.

The dashboard measures are primarily for the administration and board, and you should think hard about how best to present these to your audiences. As with any other communication, it's important to provide not only the facts but also the context and to explain what can and cannot be legitimately concluded from the data. Robert Avossa, chief accountability officer of the Charlotte-Mecklenburg Schools (a district that makes broad use of dashboards, as shown in figure 5.3[7]) makes this point strongly. "There's always a risk associated with allowing individuals to make comparisons by ZIP Code or by level, because there are assumptions made without the context," he said. "On the dashboard you're provided hard numbers, but there's a story *behind* the numbers. So we encourage people to spend time in the schools and get to know the administration and teachers." He added, "We have schools that have made unbelievable growth in recent years but they're still in the bottom third or bottom quartile. People need to understand that there are schools that are transcending typical growth expectancies, so you can't just rely on a number to tell the story."[8]

While understanding their limitations, your district can use dashboards as an opportunity to paint a fuller picture for all your district's audiences. Aside from reporting on the indicators themselves, you can discuss how and why the indicators were chosen, how they connect with overall goals, and how their results plug into the planning and implementation cycle. As we noted about financial reporting in chapter 1, bringing these kinds of topics to the attention of your audiences solidifies their impression that your district is well managed. That's a message you want them to hear over and over.

EXEMPLIFYING GOALS AND VALUES IN DISTRICT COMMUNICATIONS

In a 2003 article, educational marketer Sally Leonard described a school finance meeting at which a board member and administrators sat "half the room's length away" from the public, and at which administrators were heard to disparage community members who addressed the meeting.[9] Those behaviors send a message just as clearly as do a district's deliberate

Figure 5.3. Dashboard data samples from the Charlotte-Mecklenburg, North Carolina, school district website.

communication channels. More often than not, what school leaders *do* communicates far more than what they *say*.

Internal and external audiences alike look for signs that your district practices what it preaches. They seek evidence that you care what they think and listen to what they say. Roland Barth, founding director of the Principals' Center at Harvard University, tells the story of a doctoral candidate who visited the school where Barth was then teaching:

> I see evidence that many adults and children in the schools would like to take more risks. Yet the prevailing school culture seems preoccupied with caution. I am reminded of the doctoral candidate who came into the elementary school where I was teaching many years ago. She was writing a dissertation on the little conversation (little dance, really) that takes place when a teacher approaches a principal and asks permission to try a new idea—say, to take a field trip by boat around the Farallon Islands, seaward of the Golden Gate. Her research revealed remarkably consistent responses.
>
> The initial response of the principal was visible in body language: furrowed brow, worried look, bent shoulders. If this posture wasn't enough to stifle the idea, the next response was a litany of reasons why the idea would not work: "What about the other fourth grade across the hall? How does this fit into the scope and sequence of the required curriculum? The last time we took a field trip by boat two children got seasick, and I'm still hearing from the school board." We all know the list.
>
> If the beleaguered teacher still retains her enthusiasm, the principal's net response is, "Well, let me think about it. Get back to me in a couple of weeks." Stall. Should the teacher, somehow undeterred, return in a couple of weeks, she is then apt to hear, "Okay, you may take the field trip. But if anything happens, I want you to know it's your responsibility."
>
> Such an extraordinarily discouraging series of responses is, of course, not confined to the relations between teachers and principals. It's what the principal who wants to develop a new pupil evaluation system hears from the superintendent; it's what the student who wants to interview merchants in the neighborhood (rather than read books) for his social studies report hears from the teacher. This pathologically cautious behavior is endemic in our schools. What kind of climate for risk-taking—and therefore for learning—are we promoting with these responses to new ideas? A healthy climate for mushrooms, perhaps, but not for a community of learners.[10]

Besides demonstrating that you are listening, personal communication can show the simple value of treating everyone with respect—not only in what you say but also in how you say it. Fred Brill, superintendent in Lafayette, California, related an incident from his own experience. "As a principal, I had a parent leader who told me, 'You are not doing a good enough job challenging girls in middle school. You are shortchanging girls.'"

Brill set up a meeting with the parent leader. "I did my due diligence and gathered hordes and hordes of data, and what I found was that our girls were outperforming the boys in every single area—the number taking algebra, more girls participating in after-school activities, the number of speakers at graduation, the number of kids in after-school sports. Every single criterion that I was able to find illustrated how well the girls were doing compared to the boys. What I did foolishly, stupidly, was I compiled the data for her, put it together in a nice little packet, and very smugly plopped it down on the table. And as she was reading it I told her that the district was shortchanging the boys, and that we needed to do something about it."

"Even though I was right, I humiliated her. I created an enemy," Brill said. "Rather than engaging her in dialogue, I shut her down, and I didn't listen to where her concerns were coming from. What that meant was that I had somebody for the remainder of my tenure as principal who was looking to get me, waiting to get me." Brill sums up what he learned this way: "Don't ever treat anyone badly."[11]

Reaching Out to the Community

In contrast to the behaviors described above, leaders can demonstrate the values of listening and seeking input and involvement by going directly to community members to communicate.

In 2003, Carlos Azcoitia resigned as deputy chief of education for Chicago Public Schools and returned to Spry Elementary School, where he had once been principal, to transform it into a comprehensive preschool-through-high-school community program. His mission was to improve student achievement by forging strong partnerships with teachers, parents, and community members and ensuring "a seamless connection between what classroom teachers do during traditional school hours and what happens after school."[12] Strategies to develop these partnerships included encouraging youth and parent leadership, creating student internships in the school and community, helping organize and design a community playlot, raising funds to assist undocumented students with postsecondary goals, opening a family health clinic at the school, creating partnerships with universities, organizing an effort to press for a local branch library, and providing General Educational Development (GED), technology, and English as a second language (ESL) classes for parents. The goal was ambitious given Spry's high-poverty neighborhood, where 100 percent of the students were Hispanic and low income.

One of Azcoitia's initiatives was to involve parents through what he called the "9/9/9 Outreach Program." Nine parent leaders on nine city blocks each invited nine other parents to an evening meeting in their home. Teachers volunteered to facilitate the meetings, and topics included literacy, bilingualism, safety, health, and securing resources and information for the parents in areas such as immigration rights, neighborhood improvement, financial education, and community safety. Every family who hosted a meeting was responsible for coming up with a follow-up plan for subsequent ones.

Azcoitia believed he needed to link the school with the community and influence "the external environment"—in this case, the parents and the community. Within a year, Azcoitia and his staff involved hospitals, neighborhood youth organizations, law firms, churches, public libraries, the alderman's office, private businesses, community colleges, and banks in his outreach and support efforts.

Spry Community Links High School graduated its first class of thirty-two students in 2006 and now graduates two hundred students a year. In 2006, 97 percent of students received diplomas, with 90 percent going on to college. The school has continued to maintain high graduation and college enrollment rates.

Another school leader who "took the show on the road," this time in a wealthy suburban community, was Dick Streedain, whose strategy for building trust by involving his faculty in problem solving was discussed in chapter 2. To strengthen communication with the community, Streedain and his teachers went together to parents' homes in the evenings to talk about their work. Every Tuesday evening for three weeks, Streedain and five teachers from a grade level met with as many as sixty parents in one of their homes. They talked about their hopes for the school and discussed topics such as the best way to teach spelling. Streedain shared current research and best practices with the parent group, and the teachers explained how they applied this work in their classrooms. Some parents were surprised that Streedain was able to explain the research so clearly, noting, "This guy really knows what he's talking about!"[13]

Engaging the Community

In fall 2009, a district in the Chicago suburbs held a community meeting as part of a feasibility study on the merits of converting two K–8 buildings and one middle school into grade-level centers. The district, which had employed neighborhood schools since its inception, sought the reconfiguration to allocate resources more effectively and to improve teaching and learning for all its students, regardless of demographic characteristics, language, or where they lived within the district.

More than two hundred community and staff members packed the gymnasium, wrote their questions and comments, and had them read aloud by an outside facilitator. During the hour, none of the comments expressed support for the reconfiguration. The superintendent did not speak, nor was there an explanation of why the reconfiguration was desirable.

The district had used other avenues to explain its plan at other times, but on this night, it failed to do so with an engaged audience. The district had a chance to spend some of its "trust account" balance (chapter 2), build on any earlier communications it might have had, and make its case for the reconfiguration to community members who took the time to come to the meeting and were in a position to persuade their families, friends, and neighbors. The district listened but missed an opportunity to engage in valuable two-way communication.

Such a missed opportunity illustrates a point made by education researchers Adam Kernan-Schloss and Andy Plattner: community engagement is harder than it looks. "The public doesn't demand miracles, just progress. In most communities, the public is ready to support educational leaders who can tell them what progress they will see and when they will see it, and then report the results. Good public engagement is just that simple—and just that difficult."[14]

Difficult though it may be, districts that succeed in such efforts can find significant reward. Twin Rivers Unified School District in Sacramento County, California (see chapter 3), created a facilities advisory committee in 2009 to face issues created by budget cuts, declining enrollment, and the merger of four districts into one. The committee of community stakeholders analyzed facility and enrollment data, made preliminary recommendations, and held six forums to hear from the community at large.

Many in the new district had little or no experience with providing input at public school meetings, and some were convinced the district would proceed without caring what outsiders had to say. They wanted administrators to share details the administrators didn't have at the time the community forums were being held. School leaders did not anticipate this reaction and had to work hard to provide the information while forging new relationships with the new district's diverse subgroups. It's been a learning experience both for the district and for the community.

Twin Rivers superintendent Frank Porter noted, "We've generated some new ideas that have come out of these forums. The acid test for us is to utilize their input to refine and revise the preliminary recommendations into final recommendations. If we do it well, it's going to mobilize the community to actually commit to these newly revised proposals, because they have been involved in critiquing them and committing to some new plans. And we now have momentum to move forward."[15]

The Colorado Association of School Boards (CASB) found some similar issues in a study of community engagement that was reported on by the Kettering Foundation. The CASB looked at efforts by five school districts to improve their community relations and, in three of the five, found that no change occurred, largely because the districts were perceived to have treated public input perfunctorily. The story was different in the other two communities in the study. In one, community concerns about crime and safety led the district to hold further public forums and to seek the community's help in addressing the problem. In the other, the superintendent found new ways for the board and underrepresented segments of the community to connect, which led to changes in policy and curriculum. As Alice Diebel of the Kettering Foundation noted, "When given a chance to engage authentically in decision making, the public is likely to step up to the plate."[16]

Engaging the Staff

Your district's internal audiences are watching your communication practices as closely as your external ones are. They need to be addressed just as carefully and thoughtfully as do your families and taxpayers.

For example, the success of a new initiative might depend not on the merits of the initiative itself but on the quality of the communication that goes with it. Many districts in recent years have attempted to shape their teaching staffs into PLCs. The literature on PLCs emphasizes shared vision, shared leadership and decision making, and shared practice and collective inquiry—all of which require effective communication. Respected authors Robert Marzano, Timothy Waters, and Brian McNulty write, "This [communication] responsibility seems self-evident—good communication is a critical feature of any endeavor in which people work in close proximity for a common purpose."[17]

Your district may create structures and processes straight out of the PLC playbook, but you must still communicate effectively with the staff about changes to their working environment and behaviors, and help them communicate with students, parents, and each other. Milbrey McLaughlin and Joan Talbert studied how PLCs mature and found that teachers had to develop a "shared language, or a 'community of explanation' through which teachers could come to common understandings about teaching and learning."[18] To become a high-functioning PLC, your district has to help teachers answer questions such as the following: What language do you use to build consensus? How do you disagree with a colleague? What questions do you ask to help your colleagues evaluate and reflect upon their instructional or leadership practices? What protocols can be used to further high levels of communication?[19]

Whether you're engaged in a new initiative or not, your district can demonstrate that it is listening and learning by changing structures when needed.

In our district, building leadership teams (BLTs) were established in each school more than ten years ago to involve teachers in decision making on issues such as scheduling, planning major events, and discipline. But as district staff members became more experienced and knowledgeable about the work of professional learning communities, it became apparent that the BLTs needed to be reorganized. Teachers who served on the BLTs had a voice, but all grades, subjects, and special areas were not well represented. Areas and topics discussed by the group did not always address student learning and often focused only on surface issues.

In 2008, the district restructured the BLTs to ensure that all constituencies were heard and that the work of the BLTs would focus on substantive issues related to teaching and learning. For example, formative assessment was the focus for an entire year's professional development activities. BLT members lead that initiative, learning more about specific assessment systems through book chats and designing related activities for the whole staff. BLT members are also responsible for evaluating the effectiveness of those activities. They have a voice and their work is critical to achieving the district's strategic goals.

An example of stakeholders not given a voice in issues of importance was depicted in a 2009 PBS documentary, *The Principal Story*.[20] Over six years, Kerry Purcell, one of the principals featured, had built strong relationships with the local community, the teachers, and her students. However, without notice to her or the faculty, who traditionally had had a voice in principal selection, the superintendent decided to move her from an elementary school to a middle school. It appeared in the film that Purcell had no voice in this decision, and she was distraught at the thought of leaving her school. "This is just where I belong. I can't imagine going anywhere else. . . . This is my home and these are my family members."

The superintendent explained that, due to a mandated restructuring, "we had to really look at our best fit and put our best talent with some of our greatest needs." Unfortunately, neither Purcell nor any other stakeholders appeared to have been consulted or even informed before the decision was made by the district office. Ultimately, she decided not to take the position in the middle school and left the school system. She became a consultant training teacher leaders and principals across the country.

By not giving Purcell a voice in the decision-making process, the district lost an effective leader. Research on quality workplaces and high-functioning professional learning communities supports the importance of involving stakeholders in the decisions that affect them.

Managing the Voices

While we argue for listening to and involving stakeholders, we do not believe leaders should abdicate their responsibility to lead and make decisions. But it is critical for school leaders to communicate who bears ultimate responsibility for decisions and to make it clear what role stakeholders will have. Are they serving in an advisory capacity? Are they gathering information? In a particular instance, is the principal or the superintendent going to have the final say? If not, who is?

Stephen R. Covey talks about the importance of clarifying expectations: "If you study the underlying roots of almost all communication breakdowns, or broken, sick cultures, you'll find they come from either ambiguous or broken expectations around rules and goals."[21]

In a suburb near Chicago, more than a hundred people came to a public meeting called specifically to get community input on what should be cut from the budget. At the meeting, attendees received information about why cuts were necessary and how much needed to be trimmed, and were invited to speak directly to the board about their priorities. However, district administrators gave no public indication about which programs they were considering for trimming. Most speakers urged that two particular curricular items (full-day kindergarten and the gifted program) not be cut, but none offered any suggestions on items that could be reduced or eliminated.

In this case, the board and administration asked community members an open-ended question: what would you like to tell us about the budget? They got what they asked for. Aside from the support demonstrated for two programs, the district received no guidance from attendees about how to reduce spending. Questions that are general nearly always yield general answers, as pollsters and classroom teachers know.

You're more likely to have a productive discussion by stating what you plan to cut (with some supporting material at hand to answer questions) and asking those who attend the meeting whether they agree. If they don't, ask them what they would substitute. Framing it this way makes it more likely that those in your audience will provide useful input, and you should know where you stand when the meeting is over.

In putting tough questions before the public, school leaders may fear that, if they make their preferences known, they unfairly influence the discussion and will draw criticism for not being open to the community's views. But you are expected to have opinions about what the district should do, and you shouldn't hold back. School leaders should have enough confidence in their professional judgment to make their opinions known and enough faith in their communication skills to listen and, at times, be persuaded by the good arguments of others.

Chapter 5 Key Ideas

- Your district's goals and values provide the context and content for your communications.
- Align your messages with your goals and values.
- Develop and deliver a message that becomes your district's "brand" or identity.
- When reporting on your initiatives and discussing what's working, also share what's not working and what you're going to do about it.

Reflections

- What practices has your district used to align its communications with its goals and values?

Practices Your District Could Use to Align Its Communications with Its Goals and Values

- Bring the vision, mission, or guiding principles into the discussion when making decisions about matters large and small—not only in the budget but also in building the middle school schedule, for example.

- Put the vision and mission statements or guiding principles "front and center" when explaining to your audiences why and how decisions were made.
- Through your internal communications, consensus building, and message development sessions, get board members and administrators to agree about what your messages should be. That way, your school leaders all communicate the same information to the public.
- Consider taking your messages "on the road" occasionally. Talking to your stakeholders on their turf, not yours, can make them more comfortable and more receptive to what you have to say.

6

SHOW, DON'T TELL

Good communications—particularly good examples and stories—draw the community closer to the schools.

Policymakers can analyze data, but school leaders must focus on the real stories of real children. These stories tell your stakeholders that you are in touch with them on a personal level, reassure them that you have an emotional response to their needs and allow you to build a bridge between your emotions and their emotions. In the end most stakeholders vote with their heart and not their head.

—Jennifer Laszlo Mizrahi and Talton Gibson[1]

How your district talks about itself—its issues, merits, and demerits—has a bearing on how it will be perceived by its audiences. In our view, one of the fundamental tenets of how a district can most effectively tell its story is this: show, don't tell.

There are two key components to this strategy. One is to emphasize facts (show) over assertions (tell). The other is to use examples, analogies, and real-life experiences in your district's communications. By showing what you are doing, you help your audiences understand your district.

Teachers do this all the time. They talk their students through sample problems to illustrate math concepts; they compare the statements or actions of one historical figure to another to highlight similarities or differences in their political philosophies; they perform experiments in front of the class to demonstrate principles of physics or chemistry. Their purpose in doing so is the same as yours in directing district communication—to give audiences information they will retain and use. In your case, you want the community to understand your goals and values, and to be educated about your district's processes and activities. You need communications that give your audiences the context for your district's decisions, and you want your community to use that information to act in ways that benefit the district.

For example, if your district uses the dashboard metaphor for the details the board and community want to focus on (see chapter 5), that provides specific guidance on the kinds of stories you want to tell. The dashboard—a set of specific factual indicators that, taken together, provide a snapshot of the district's progress at any given moment—tells everyone the "what" about how the district is doing. But the underlying stories telling the "how" and "why" are equally important. Data and trend analysis can't be ignored, but teachers talking about how a particular book, practice, or other curriculum component helps them connect with students, or students talking about how important a coach or drama teacher is to them, really has impact. In the same way that, as Roland Barth noted, "careful use of storytelling can promote profound levels of learning by leaders,"[2] it can also turn dry policy discussions into clear, compelling narratives.

MAKE YOUR CASE

As in chapter 1, we make a distinction between basic information that your district is required to disseminate and additional information that helps you nurture community support. You are not going to use examples or analogies in your school calendar. But often, districts behave as though putting out routine descriptive information about a program or initiative is all that needs to be done. That's just the beginning.

Research into persuasive communication tells us something about the kinds of communication that help—or hurt—organizations. Some of that research indicates, not surprisingly, that the more involved in an issue or organization an audience member feels, the more time he or she is willing to devote to considering information about it.[3] The more detailed a presentation is, the more persuasive it is likely to be—and the more likely it is that an involved person (such as a parent, teacher, or taxpayer during a referendum campaign) will take the time to read or listen to it.

However, that research also shows that poorly executed communications can alienate even your most involved audiences. If your communications are boring, slapdash, or raise more questions than they answer, they may not get the credence you think they deserve. That's why advertisers and political figures work as hard on crafting their messages as they do on finding attractive and likable messengers to deliver them.

On the other hand, those who do not feel involved are much less willing to pay attention to attempts to persuade. They are the ones who are likely to be turned off by "too much information." Your district needs to hit the highlights and make the details available only to those who really want them. For example, District 145 in Freeport, Illinois, distributes its annual strategic plan as a "plan on a page"—a single sheet of paper.[4]

Your district should address your more distant audiences in ways that encourage them to be more involved. You can do that with communications that have memorable, focused messages; that repeat those messages in different ways; and that provide examples they can relate to—that put them in the shoes of your teachers, students, or families. Through communications like these, you draw them closer to your district. And the closer they feel, the more likely they are to pay attention to your messages and act on them.

LET FACTS TELL THE STORY

When a committee of administrators and teachers in our district was preparing our middle school's application for the U.S. Department of Education's Blue Ribbon of Excellence in 2001, the initial draft had plenty of strong sounding assertions but not enough factual support. By the time we submitted the application, however, that support was in place. Instead of statements that asserted faculty members were highly involved in curriculum and initiatives, for example, we wrote that more than 90 percent of the teaching staff was involved in curriculum and program committees.

We got the award.

In the same vein, reporting a high percentage of teacher-family contact makes a more persuasive impression than merely saying that teachers do a good job of keeping in touch with families. Noting the exact number of your district's teachers who hold advanced degrees, including National Board Certification (assuming it's a high percentage), makes a better argument than "our teachers are highly qualified." Unsupported generalities leave the uncomfortable implication that the district will not—or cannot—back up its assertions with facts. By laying out the details, your district makes it clear that you know your numbers and that they support your arguments.

One of the most compelling ways to let the facts speak for themselves (and also to provide examples) is to display student work. Most school hallways, of course, are festooned with student-created banners and artwork—because the district wants those efforts to be displayed, and parents really like it. But how often do otherwise uninvolved members of your school community get to see those displays? What kind of impact do you think it would have if they did?

And your public displays aren't restricted to artwork. Science or technology fairs, at which students display what they've learned, are another venue for presenting the facts of student achievement. So are music or theater performances, and athletic events. All of these are opportunities for your students to demonstrate what they've learned, what they can do, and what they've been taught by your staff. Some districts even make a point of explicitly connecting student work that is displayed with the associated learning standards.

Your district should display student work as broadly as possible—that's one of the best uses of your Web operation, for example. Encourage your students to create lots of content, using sound and images as well as words. Beyond the Web, city halls and public libraries often offer venues for public display, as may your community's local media outlets. When your students' work appears in those settings, there's significant benefit in making your community aware of it. Almost anything that involves children draws attendance and attention. Take advantage of that.

DRIVE THE POINT HOME

Facts are essential. But real stories with real people are credible and persuasive. Your audiences can relate to teachers, students, or families who have something interesting to say about what you do. By choosing your examples truthfully and carefully, your district makes the most effective arguments in favor of its programs.

Our district adopted "The Daily Five" literacy program—a curriculum that helps students "develop the daily habits of reading, writing, and working independently"—in its early elementary grades.[5] An article in the district's community newsletter about the program explained how it works but didn't dwell on the rationale behind it. Rather, it emphasized how teachers (many of whom spent some of their own money to get training) found their young students responding to the change.

"I can really focus more on the teaching of reading—they know the behavioral expectations and the common language. They're excited that they know what to do," said one first-grade teacher. "They're really motivated and enjoy reading and writing. My kids are held accountable for their learning—I'm monitoring their progress, and they're monitoring their progress at the same time," said a second-grade teacher.[6]

Conveying the enthusiasm of students and teachers for a curriculum change tells a different—and better—story than droning on about test scores and pedagogy. Scores need to be reported, of course, and being able to explain the educational reasons for a particular curriculum component is necessary. But personal stories involve and connect your audiences with your district. And that's the goal of communications.

VARY YOUR CONTENT

Another way of showing instead of telling in your district's communications is to use images and sound as well as words. Photos, illustrations, audio, and video can present both facts and examples. They also carry information in different ways than text does and can better reach those in your audience who learn better by hearing or seeing than reading.

Use of multimedia will only be more common as time goes on. Now that anyone with a cell phone has the ability to take pictures, or record sound and video images, they are proliferating. While perhaps not all files captured this way deserve an audience, they are becoming not only common but also expected, particularly among younger audiences.

We'll discuss this further in chapter 8, but here are a few things to keep in mind when deciding how to use images and sound:

Maintain some quality standards. Blurry photos, unintelligible sound, or motion-sickness-inducing videos don't help you communicate.

Less really is more. Pick a few of the best images to accompany your Web story and only one or two for the newsletter. By all means, take a lot of photos when the situation warrants. Just don't plan to display them all. A few well-chosen shots can convey your message while not overloading your audience.

Encourage participation. Find out who among your staff likes to take photos or videos and ask them to contribute to your publications or website. Recruit students to help provide your content.

Use good judgment. Not everyone has a trained eye or ear, but as an experienced school leader, you have a sense of what's appropriate, what tells the story, and what doesn't. If you find you're shooting down more ideas than you're approving (or vice versa), ask your colleagues what they think. Your district could even put together a small, informal review committee for content if necessary.

LEARN FROM EXAMPLES

Just as you want to educate your audiences by providing examples, you can take advantage of that process yourself. There are times when your local newspaper or television station will do a story about your district that conveys just what you hope it will. Whether that happens frequently or not—and regardless of what you may do to facilitate it—your district can learn from those instances. After all, "show, don't tell" is axiomatic in journalism classrooms and newsrooms everywhere.

Any competent journalist will employ the same techniques we recommend here: to build a story using a telling example and marshaling details to paint an accurate overall picture. Look at news stories (particularly longer features) that strike you as good models, break them down, and emulate them in your district's own storytelling.

In that same vein, you can be on the lookout for good stories that other school districts tell. Information about most of the world's districts is only a couple of clicks away, and your district can take advantage of that. If there's an issue, or a type of story, that you want to convey, put the topic into a search engine and see what you find. Look at the examples those other districts cite; look at whether (and how) they integrate images or sound or video; and look at stories that really stand out.

Don't waste time with the examples that make you shrug your shoulders. Home in on those that have an impact on you—good or bad. You can learn what to do from the good examples and what not to do from the bad.

Chapter 6 Key Ideas

- Give your community more information than the minimum required.
- When communicating to your audiences, use facts to support generalizations about concepts such as quality staff, fiscal responsibility, and exceptional student performance.
- Drive your points home with stories about the impact various programs have on students, teachers, and others.

Reflections

- What practices has your district used to show, rather than merely tell?

Practices Your District Could Use to Show, Rather Than Merely Tell

- In newsletter and Web articles, let teachers and students explain how programs or initiatives have affected them.
- In your budget narrative, give examples of ways priorities have changed from year to year; explain why they changed.
- Provide parents with before-and-after data comparing students' actual growth with expectations after participating in a new program.

7

CULTIVATE CREDIBILITY

School communications must be credible to be effective.

Credibility is vital to all public administration professionals. We are the ones, of course, on whom elected and appointed officials, as well as the public, depend to analyze problems, research issues, develop solutions, and tell the truth about what the results and potential consequences are. Building credibility allows you to "tell your story" to a variety of stakeholders, even if they disagree with your position.

—Irene Navis[1]

The success of your district's communications depends, among other things, on the extent to which your audiences believe what you're saying. You can craft messages carefully, present them effectively, use the right channels, reach the right people, and still fail—if those who hear and see the messages don't buy them.

Your credibility, along with competence and good intent, are the factors that determine whether your audience will trust your district's communications (see chapter 2). In this chapter, we will cover strategies and tactics that enhance the credibility of communications.

DEFINING CREDIBILITY

Stephen M. R. Covey defines credibility in terms of four cores or factors: integrity, intent, capabilities, and results. He quotes the vice president of marketing at a large company about the company's desire to be credible as an organization: "'We need to ensure that customers understand our reputation around integrity. We need to declare our intent to help them win. We need to show them our capabilities to add value to their organization. We need to demonstrate our results and track record to them so that they will stay with us.'"[2]

Your district's communications should work toward those same ends, rather than focusing solely on results, as many school communications seem to do. Letting your audiences know *why* and *how* things are being done, as well as *what* is being done, can provide insight into your district's integrity, intent, and capabilities. When you discuss student achievement, for example, you can talk about more than test scores—you can talk about instructional practices your teachers used, a new curriculum, extended-day programs, summer school, tutoring, or a professional development initiative. You can talk about how school leaders chose their strategies to raise those scores and what the staff's capacity is (not only in numbers but also in skills and abilities) to carry them out.

When our district sought community support to build an addition to its middle school, we promised that the addition would incorporate sound environmental practices. When it was completed, in 2009, the community was invited in to see the addition's green roof, solar panels, motion-sensitive lighting, and dual-flush toilets, as well as to observe the new and improved instructional spaces. Our communications have since discussed the ways the green addition has benefited the district and how teachers and students are learning from them.

By communicating about the details of the addition, our district has been able to display integrity and intent by showing that school leaders worked to save money (through energy savings), help the environment (by reducing energy use and reusing materials where possible), and keep its promises (by delivering on the promise of green building practices).

BEHAVING CREDIBLY

Some key leadership and communications practices can enhance your district's credibility. (As Covey notes, they align with practices that leaders can use to engender trust.[3]) These include standing by commitments, communicating openly and honestly, telling the whole story, and listening.

Standing by Commitments

In 1993, Griff Powell was superintendent of Highwood-Highland Park School District 111, which served about five hundred mostly minority students from a neighboring military base as well as children from working-class Italian and Mexican immigrant families. The two neighboring school districts in Highland Park, a wealthy Chicago suburb, served primarily nonminority students from high-income families and benefited from a rich property tax base.

When District 111 faced serious budget cuts, Powell decided to push for consolidation. In the campaign, opponents accused him of orchestrating the merger so he could take over as superintendent of the new, larger district. He responded by pledging not to remain with the district if voters approved the consolidation. In summer 1993, the referendum passed, and in November, Powell took a job as superintendent in New York State—to the chagrin of his children, who were in elementary school at the time and had to relocate. Nevertheless, Powell stood by his promise.[4]

Conversely, an example of a failure to keep a commitment was reported by the Colorado Association of School Boards (CASB) in its 2003 study of community engagement referred to in chapter 5. In one of the districts studied, the school board promised "it would not take any action on the proposed closures or school consolidations until after the board had listened in on the community conversations." But in response to an unanticipated five-million-dollar budget shortfall, the board chose to consolidate three schools without the community input it had promised. The CASB analysis concluded that the board dealt with its financial crisis as it had with other crises—"in isolation and without any consultation or engagement with its publics. Had the board used the unexpected financial circumstances as an opportunity to extend and broaden its conversation with its publics, a very different relationship with its publics may have been nurtured and some first steps toward a fundamentally new approach to decision making may have been begun."[5]

Communicating Openly and Honestly

In chapter 1, we acknowledged that perhaps not all school leaders agree that "honesty is the best policy" but still argued for openness. In that spirit, in our district we scheduled a public hearing on our proposed property tax levy, even though the proposed tax increase was below the state-mandated threshold above which a hearing is required. Our business manager believed there should be a hearing anyway; she wanted to be "completely transparent" and available for questions from the public.[6]

Another district learned the value of transparency in much more trying circumstances. Charlotte-Mecklenburg Schools in North Carolina, a district that has received the National School Public Relations Association (NSPRA) Gold Medallion Award for public relations, lost a $457 million construction-bond vote in 2005. Surveys following the defeat "revealed widespread dissatisfaction with the school board and district leadership and deep concerns about fiscal management."[7] The district regrouped, and under the leadership of a new superintendent, Peter Gorman, launched a campaign to demonstrate more openness in the district.

When there was an incident involving a teacher accused of taking drugs in school, "Gorman held a press conference, expressing not just his outrage about what had happened but also explaining how it had happened and how the district would avoid similar situations in the future." Gorman said the press conference "sent a strong message about transparency." By 2006, polls indicated approval for the new superintendent's methods. Nora Carr, chief communications officer, said of the outreach efforts, "It wasn't a program so much as a change of culture. . . . We made a concerted effort to be transparent, to make all of the decision-making processes and all of the decisions as public as possible."[8]

Telling the Whole Story

Every school leader knows to tell the truth, but telling the whole truth is not always easy. It's natural to want to emphasize the positive and leave out the negative in your district's communications. However, to do so severely harms the district's credibility. If you're perceived as only telling the good news, your community begins to doubt, and pay less attention to, what you're saying.

The biggest risk to telling only half the story is that the other half will eventually come out—the most damaging scenario to your district's credibility, since the public not only learns the bad news but also gets the sense that you were trying to hide it. You're always better off assuming that, when bad news happens, everyone will find out. It's best they find out from you. You have one chance to give your version of the story unencumbered by the versions of others—that's by telling it first.

Bill Berg, a former Chicago TV and radio broadcaster, gave this advice about crisis situations, but it applies even in less difficult circumstances.

"Everybody knows there is a crisis. Any obvious attempt to gloss over the serious nature of the situation will be met with harsh criticism from both the press and the public. It is much better to acknowledge the severity of the crisis with accurate information."[9]

One day early in the 2003 school year, officials in our district discovered that a preschooler had accidentally been left locked in a school bus for about three hours. This happened because of a series of failures to follow procedure, which is often the case when something bad happens. Once we discovered what happened, and determined that the child was unharmed, we had to decide how to communicate with parents and the public about this incident.

In the days before e-mails and automated phone calls were common, we would typically send a letter home to families in an event such as this. The letter was prepared to be sent the next day. However, school officials were divided on what other steps to take—one wanted to send a press release to major local media outlets explaining what happened, and what the district's plans were for ensuring that it would not happen again. Others opposed the idea, hoping the story wouldn't go beyond those who already knew about it. The release was written but not sent immediately.

The point became moot that evening, when the superintendent got a call from a Chicago TV news producer following up on a tip he had received about a child left on a bus. She asked the producer if he would like a copy of their press release and he said, in effect, "You bet I would!" The superintendent faxed the release to the producer and agreed to be interviewed. The press release was the district's version of what happened, not someone else's interpretation. There were two days of news stories about the incident, but after that, the story disappeared.

We were able to explain the incident, take responsibility for seeing that similar ones would not happen again, and move on. We had to make a withdrawal from our trust bank but were able to maintain our credibility—which would have been seriously threatened if school officials had attempted to deny what happened or even if they had simply chosen not to comment when the reporter called. In this case, a "no comment" would likely have been just as damaging as a denial, since the story would then have run without the district's explanation.

We also learned that next time (if there were to be one, and so far there hasn't), we would not wait for the reporter's call before telling the whole story. Our district would be better off following the example of U.S. Air Force secretary Michael Wynne, who, rather than hiding his agency's mistake, called a press conference to explain it (see box on page 18, chapter 2).

Besides communicating with the public at large, our district had to address this issue directly with the parents of our preschoolers. We did so by quickly convening a meeting at which we gave them as much information as we could—which wasn't everything, because school officials were still investigating when the meeting took place. Nevertheless, we felt strongly that we needed to explain as much as we reasonably could, while—perhaps more importantly—giving these parents a chance to ask their questions and express their concerns. School leaders recognized that most of the parents were very frightened since this was their first experience dealing with a school district, no prior relationships had been established, and consequently, there was no balance in the trust bank. The superintendent attempted to allay their fears and told parents there was no time limit on the meeting that night and that she would stay until every question had been asked and answered.

It was a difficult but necessary meeting. The superintendent pledged to do all she could to prevent a repeat incident, and parents were able to—in no uncertain terms—let the district know how they felt. Aside from relating the facts, the district was able to communicate its intent and demonstrate its capacity to listen.

As an unintended but welcome side benefit, there was a man at the meeting whose children were not yet old enough for preschool. He had heard about the meeting and wanted to check out the district and the situation. He asked great questions and offered wonderful suggestions and, years later, was elected to the school board, where he is a valued member.

One last point—your district can't tell the whole story if some concepts or ideas are out of bounds. In December 2009, the *Wall Street Journal* reported an example of the latter that came from a news organization. *Gulf News*, the largest English-language daily in the United Arab Emirates, was reported to have banned the use of the words "bailout" and "default" in writing about the debt crisis in Dubai.[10] In your district, are there words or phrases that the community isn't allowed to hear?

Listening

We discussed the importance of understanding your audiences in chapter 4. To gain that understanding, your district has to create opportunities to listen to them. By doing so, the district not only gains knowledge it needs to communicate effectively—it also enhances its credibility by demonstrating the willingness to find out what's happening, what's working, and what's not, and by responding accordingly. (See chapters 4 and 9 for some tactics to help your district listen better.)

One example comes from Schaumburg, Illinois, where Superintendent Ed Rafferty uses "board communication teams" to incorporate listening into his district's internal communications. Each board member meets with teachers and a support staff member selected by the union. These teams allow the board and administration to understand the wants, needs, and concerns of the union members, and to advocate for the interests of the board and administration.

Rafferty adds individual communications to his union relations by speaking with union leadership daily. He also attends their monthly executive meetings where union representatives can ask about anything. He said, "We haven't had a formal grievance since the early '70s, because we can pretty much work things out."

Broadening employee communications beyond the union, Rafferty also established a "superintendent's communication council." The council meets five times a year, and each of the twenty-seven schools in the district selects its own representative—anyone from the school custodian to the head teacher. To build the agenda, the director of communications asks the representatives what they would like to discuss. Rafferty answers every question on the agenda, and meeting notes are published for every staff member.[11]

Here's an example of building listening into external communications. At Orono Public Schools in Long Lake, Minnesota, efforts to listen to the community grew out of a failed attempt to increase funding for operations, technology, and facility improvements in 2005. Superintendent Karen Orcutt noted that "it was obvious that there was a great deal of confusion about Orono and that we didn't fully understand the community or it understand us. . . . I had a million opinions on my desk, but I realized I had to first find out what was going on at a deeper level."[12]

The district (which received the Gold Medallion Award from NSPRA in 2008) set up community coffees, superintendent home visits, and meetings with stakeholders including the clergy, local businesses, parents, and students. Orcutt recalled, "I went everywhere, listened to everybody. I stayed as long as people wanted to talk, and I listened very hard." In February 2008, the district's facilities referendum passed.

Chapter 7 Key Ideas

- Stand by your commitments.
- Communicate openly and honestly.

- Always tell as much as you can; when some information cannot be revealed (matters of privacy or sensitive negotiations, for example), explain why it cannot be discussed.
- There's no use trying to hide bad news; it will come out eventually.
- By telling your stakeholders about it first, you can explain what happened and head off misinformation before it spreads.

Reflections

- What practices has your district used to build credibility?

Practices Your District Could Use to Build Credibility

- Share information with parents explaining when you made a mistake and how you rectified it; use the active voice ("We made a mistake" not "Mistakes were made"[13]).
- Take people inside the process you use to create and implement initiatives; help them understand what the challenges were and why you made particular decisions.

8

TAKE ADVANTAGE OF TECHNOLOGY

Wise use of technology allows schools to reach people more effectively, more often.

For any given organization, the important questions are, "When will the change happen?" and "What will change?" The only two answers we can rule out are never, and nothing.

—Clay Shirky[1]

The availability of a vast array of new tools is changing the communications landscape. They are changing the speed at which your district can communicate, the size of the audience you can reach, the amount of information you can cost-effectively transmit, and—most important—the expectations for communication your community members have. Your district must understand the changing technology to decide what to adopt and when.

WHAT'S CHANGING—CHANNELS AND ROLES

Let's look at what's happened to newsletters to see how communication channels and communication roles are changing. If you're old enough, think about how communications worked three decades ago, before desktop publishing. Then, you were limited by cost and by the fact that only a few people had the skills and tools necessary to produce communication vehicles. If your district had a community newsletter, someone within the district gathered information and wrote it (or gave it to an outside writer), and the project probably went to an outside designer, a printer, and a mailer. Because so much of the work was done by vendors, your district could likely afford to create and distribute these newsletters only a few times a year.

Then desktop publishing came along, offering the prospect of turning you and members of your staff into writers, editors, and publishers. If you chose to do the newsletter in-house, costs went down, even allowing for the cost of buying hardware and software and training staffers to use it. If you continued to use outside help, costs still went down due to supply and demand—the number of possible vendors was increased by fast-spreading, readily available technology. Either way, for the same money as before, you could produce more newsletters during the course of a year—or could at least keep cranking out the same number when the budget got tight.

As e-mail and the Internet have grown and evolved, your district's communications changed again. Your newsletters can now be made into PDFs, posted on your website, and advertised via e-mails. This not only drastically reduces production and distribution costs but also opens up more options. Before, newsletter photos might have been printed in black and white to avoid the cost of four-color process printing. Now the PDF can use full color, and recipients can view them on their color monitors or print out copies on their own inexpensive inkjet printers if they wish. Similarly, while the newsletter might once have been limited to four or eight pages due to the costs and constraints of commercial printing (having to print pages in multiples of four, for example), now you can create a document

> In Barrington, Illinois, one of Chicago's northern suburbs, School District 220 has made a significant commitment to electronic communications. According to Jeffrey Arnett, chief communications officer, families prefer the high-tech channels and appreciate the cost savings of reducing printed materials, but they fear they're getting too much information.
> Arnett said all the district's communicators are aware of this issue and "need to temper the volume of communication." He said most routine communications go through an administrative assistant in each of the school buildings and that those staff members—along with teachers, principals, and Parent-Teacher Organization (PTO) representatives—have received training on how to use the channels and streamline the messages.
> For his part, Arnett said he works continually on simplifying messages: "How can I condense my thoughts into a 30-second sound bite?"[2]

with the number of pages required to transmit the content, and that number could be five, nine, or fifteen. The cost is the time and manpower to create the document.

The same scenario is true for audio and video production, to name two other examples. As computers have become more powerful, and digital input devices more affordable and widespread, the old constraints on information transmission—cost and expertise—have melted away.

And the pace of change is accelerating; now, anyone with the right handheld device can become a photographer, sound engineer, videographer, or publisher. The old model of information carefully packaged into limited forms and distributed to a defined list of households or subscribers is morphing into a collection of products that might include Web links, pictures, illustrations, sound, and video, available to anyone in the world.

Desktop publishing made people into editors and publishers, while reducing expectations about absolute measures of quality. Graphic designers and printers who objected as print quality and photographic reproduction devolved to the level of laser or inkjet printing are no longer even trying. The audience that receives the newsletters has become accustomed to simple graphics or clip art and is more concerned about what the newsletter says.

In the same way, it matters less that video was shot on an inexpensive digital video camera (or even a phone) than what is shown—as long as it's not so shaky and poorly lit that it doesn't reveal anything. No one expects theater-quality sound and video from a Web clip. Does the video show an example of real student achievement? Does it demonstrate innovative teaching and learning? Does it make a point about insufficient resources? It's the content that matters.

WHAT'S CHANGING—SOCIAL NETWORKING

As author and social networking expert Shirky argues, the explosion of social networking tools has reduced or eliminated barriers that, in the past, made it hard for individuals to connect and quickly organize.[3] This has enormous implications for established organizations of all kinds, including school districts.

For one thing, school districts move from a position of controlling a substantially centralized conversation about school matters to simply trying to influence an array of decentralized conversations. For another, districts have to keep up with the rapidly changing collection of websites, applications, and devices that audiences are employing (and, increasingly, expect you to employ as well). Take so-called mommy blogs, for example—the *New York Times* has called them "a cultural force to be reckoned with."[4] Some of those moms send their children to your schools.

Conversations

The conventional conversations about school matters have changed now that attendance at a given board meeting can skyrocket unexpectedly due to community members tweeting or texting one another about a particular issue or concern, or districts can be inundated with requests for information or criticism for not making certain information available. Where before, a handful of people might take the time to make a phone call, now dozens or hundreds might be moved to send a quick e-mail, text, or forum post. Where before, someone who had a concern would not bother to place a call on the weekend, and then might forget about it or decide it's not worth it by Monday, now that person can send the message right away.

On the other hand, keep in mind that the significance of an individual message is changing. Because social networking communications cost so little in time and effort, they may not reflect the same sort of commitment on the part of your community as before. In the past, you might have assumed that, if a half-dozen people called or wrote letters about an issue, there were several times that number who shared the particular concern but didn't take the time to call or write. You can't make that same assumption about e-mails, text messages, or Twitter posts, because they're so easy to generate. You need to raise the threshold number of contacts, and pay attention to other evidence, before you decide how serious an issue those electronic messages represent.

In chapter 4 we discussed how school communities could be broken down into constituent groups. In the future, they may also be made up of communities of interest, that is, those parents and families who really care about nutrition, special education, autism, or sports. In fact, parents and families have always had such interests, but most were satisfied with what the district was doing; the ones who were not often were too few or too scattered, or weren't comfortable confronting school leaders. With social networking, the cost of organizing is so small that a group can form, and evaporate, far more easily than ever. In the past, the band boosters or the baseball parents had to at least establish enough of an organizational structure not only to pass along information, raise money, and decide who was bringing snacks to the game but also to stay alive as parents came and went. They also had to establish a relationship with the district to gain access to the students, parents, and families that organizers wanted to reach. Now, using social networking tools and working entirely outside the auspices of the district, subgroups could form to push for more (or fewer) Mozart pieces in the orchestra program, or more (or fewer) bunts by the ballplayers.[5]

Social networking among all those subgroups poses a challenge, and an opportunity, to any district that attempts to respond to and engage them. Of course, the challenge is that the district has no control over the messages that people convey to one another; they may be truthful or not, constructive or not. The opportunity is to monitor, respond, and to attempt to influence the conversations that go on—tasks that districts today ignore at their peril. The authors of OhMyGov!—a website about government issues—relate this story about quick response:

> In January of 2009 and 2010, seismologists at the United States Geologic Survey picked up on rumors originating in blogs and spread via Twitter and other social media, that Yellowstone National Park's super-volcano would soon erupt.
> Concerned about public panic fed by the rumors, officials at the USGS and Yellowstone National Park updated their social media pages with factual explanations of the seismic activity in order to combat the fearmongering. The direct response was uncharacteristic, as government agencies generally prefer to address rumors indirectly, so as not to give further attention or credence to the posters.
> But here, Yellowstone park officials linked a tweet to their Facebook page, which included a longer description of the occurring seismic activity, along with a special message that read: "NOTE: Don't fret; University of Utah researchers remind the public that earthquakes are a common event in the world's first national park."
> The USGS added its own response, linking a tweet to a previously written article about earthquake swarms on its website, which also stressed the normality of seismic activity in Yellowstone.
> Together, the "official" links provided some facts and critical context to those stricken with fear or mere curiosity about the rumbles in the ground. Citizens reading these official accounts by @USGS or @ynp tweeted the good word that Yellowstone was no more active than it had been (on average) in the past, putting an end to the rumor of imminent catastrophe.
> Dina Venezky, a USGS staff member working at the University of Utah's Yellowstone Volcano Observatory, said of the swarm rumors, "It appeared that many people helped dispel misinformation quickly, which

we greatly appreciated and attributed to our increased communications over the past few years."[6]

Keeping Up

As the number of people using social networking tools grows, so does the expectation that your district will be using them to communicate. Parents who prefer school communications on paper are aging out of your schools and being replaced by those who assume communications will be electronic and who expect a menu of choices so that they can control how they receive information. The next wave—which may already have arrived—will be parents who have never experienced communications any other way.

This is true for your staff as well, not to mention the community at large. But because those groups don't pass through as quickly as parents, more of them must be addressed using the entire range of communications tools—you can't yet get rid of paper communications altogether. Like the rest of society, your school community is in transition from the old communications to the new, and that transition is going to go on for quite some time—to an end that no one can predict.

However, it's obvious at this point that (at least in relation to technology) what starts out as possible soon becomes expected, then necessary. More and more, school districts are finding this out and responding—as the Salt Lake City school district did in 2009 when it established a presence on Twitter and Facebook. Jason Olsen, district communications officer, said, "Many organizations, businesses and everything else have been moving in that direction, so our parents were expecting the same sort of response, the same notification process that they get from other places."[7]

There are more examples every day of ways organizations in general, and school districts in particular, are using technology to communicate. Art teachers in Utah use Internet tools to allow students to share ideas and critiques with each other, thus creating a platform where the larger school community—not to mention the world—can view and appreciate their work.[8] The same kind of thing is happening in a Kentucky school district where all teachers have blogs. "We have a French teacher at the high school who even uses her blog to communicate with a teacher in France, and their students are communicating back and forth using the French language," said the district's tech coordinator. "I honestly don't think we expected anything like this."[9]

It is certainly not unexpected that students would embrace the technologies in school that they use so frequently in their daily lives. In a study released in 2007 by the National School Boards Association, 96 percent of students with online access reported using social networking tools.[10] It's no wonder, then, that teachers such as those mentioned above—and a legion of others—are trying to find ways to use these tools to promote teaching and learning. It only makes sense that districts show the same determination to reach not only these new generations of students but also their parents, families, and everyone else.

It is critical for your district to make social networking work in your favor. To use the new tools effectively within this uncertain environment, you must commit to the premise that communication flows both ways (from the district to its constituents and back) and use each tool appropriately (i.e., SMS or Twitter for short bursts of information and the Web, print, or face-to-face for more information and deeper discussions). Similar to the way schools must prepare students for an uncertain future, the broader challenge for school leaders is to build a communications structure flexible enough to handle that which you don't know is coming.

Engaging the Public

Municipalities and other local governments have communications issues similar to those of school districts. The city of Evanston, Illinois, for example, took a technology-savvy, integrated communications approach to its effort to bring more community participation into the difficult process of reducing its $9.5 million budget deficit.[11]

City officials scheduled public workshops at which they presented the numbers about the projected deficit and solicited suggestions from attendees about how to fix it. The workshops were broadcast on public-access television. Copious budget information, including background, trend graphs, the workshop videos, and links to supporting documents, was also housed on a dedicated set of pages within the city's website.[12] There, interested residents could read the details and vote on the proposed changes that came out of the workshops. City officials are pleased with the input they've received and say the website will remain online and continue to be used in future budget processes.

Similarly, school districts have begun posting board packets online, bringing remote speakers to classrooms via Skype or iChat, or streaming their board meetings live from their websites. A leadership coach told us about viewing a board meeting that was being videostreamed. That evening, the school principal, whom she was coaching, had to respond to an angry group of parents. As the meeting was in progress, the leadership

Figure 8.1. In Barrington, Illinois, School District 220 communicates regularly through its YouTube channel.

coach texted the principal with suggestions about how to deal with the parents. Some also have created YouTube channels that allow viewers to access their videos on demand while not having to store large files on their own servers, such as Barrington School District 220 in suburban Chicago (see figure 8.1).

Shenendehowa Central Schools, a K–12 district in southern Saratoga County, New York, that serves about ten thousand students, created a moderated blog to answer all kinds of questions from the community.[13] Called "Heard It through the Grapevine," the blog was started as a way to combat the spread of rumors by allowing people to ask a question anonymously and get an answer.

Kelly DeFeciani, the district's public information officer, explained the rationale behind the blog this way when it was created in February 2008:

> People are becoming more and more accustomed to immediate communication. It is important that the district explore every new technological tool available to communicate with the public to ensure that we

reach as many people as possible. While the Shenendehowa community is fairly large, rumors and inaccurate information spread "through the grapevine" at lightning speed. We want to reduce the "ballpark" chatter and provide a place for people to get accurate answers quickly. This venue provides anonymity so that people can feel comfortable coming directly to this district's information source rather than getting the information from their neighbor or rumor mill, which is frequently inaccurate.[14]

Along with the anonymity policy, the district applied other guidelines. Insulting comments or questions are out of bounds and will not be answered, nor will those that invade the privacy of individuals or that refer to specific persons.

The "Grapevine" was initially promoted through the district's newsletter and website, and DeFeciani also alerted district staff, the Parent-Teacher Association (PTA), and local news outlets. In the first two weeks, she said, the blog received 388 questions; in the first month, traffic on the district's website increased by one thousand unique visitors. After two full years of operation, DeFeciani said the blog receives fifty to seventy-five questions a day, and the district's website has seen its monthly visitor count go from twenty-eight thousand to more than forty-six thousand, with sixteen thousand of those attributable to the "Grapevine." She said she spends about an hour a day getting questions answered and managing the blog.

District officials believe the blog has been a smashing success. As Superintendent L. Oliver Robinson wrote in January 2010, "The district has the ability to be the first, best, and fastest source of information to the public."[15]

And the Shenendehowa community seems to agree. Here's a sampling of feedback DeFeciani has received since the blog began:

- "After reading through all of the comments, I have realized that all of your efforts go unnoticed, or worse, questioned. I would just like to say thank you for all of your hard work and truthful responses."
- "This instrument for communications is probably more important than can actually be realized."
- "Getting the facts straight on much of the 'gossip' that goes around town is very helpful."
- "I have a child in elementary school; I find the Grapevine to be a tool helping me identify issues to be aware of as my child moves from elementary school, through middle school, to high school."

- "I love the Grapevine. I spend all of my 7th periods with my friend reading them. Thank you. Have you ever considered making Grapevine shirts?"
- "I'm sure having information available at the click of a mouse to many people all at once beats answering the telephone and answering the same questions over and over to one person at a time. It seems to me that it saves time and money."
- "I don't have a question and in the past, not every question I have sent in has been answered. But—I still wanted to let you know that I think you do a fabulous job with this."
- "It may not be 'perfect' but it's a great way for parents to get a sense of what is going on. Even if I don't have a particular question, I always come here just to see what the 'buzz' is."[16]

Engaging Teachers

Besides allowing teachers to better communicate with students (as in Utah and Kentucky), and allowing districts to deliver straight talk to community members, social networking offers a host of tools that can be used to communicate with staff members and contribute to their professional development. To these ends, wikis, blogs, internal forum posts, or Twitter employ the same vital communications principle the education profession has used since its inception—allowing practitioners to share their knowledge.

Here again, your district moves from a position of controlling the conversation to influencing a cluster of conversations. You can use these tools to distribute information the district wants its staff members to have, but the conversations won't stop there. In fact, those conversations could involve anyone, anywhere, who has something to say and the yen to participate.

More and more, professional organizations are using social media tools such as Ning to allow their members to connect and share information. But as Shirky noted, it's also easier than ever for individuals to do this on their own. Nancy Stewart, a learning resource teacher in a K–8 district in suburban Chicago, finds herself in an online "community of practice" centered on teaching that not only extends beyond the borders of her district but also is international.[17] "I'm an avid Twitterer," she said. "I've basically developed a professional learning network, including special education teachers, math teachers, writing and English teachers, teachers who specialize in assistive technology. I feel like the group of people I've been able to surround myself with is a brain trust. No matter the question, they are unbelievably generous."[18]

Using resources she discovers on her own, and those passed along by others, Stewart believes she has become a better teacher. Similar to what researchers have done by networking computers to take advantage of all of their processing power (known as distributive computing), her linked network takes advantage of the most powerful processors known to man—human brains. "Five years ago, I was going and finding information, evaluating it, and coming back to my work. Now, I have others who can evaluate, recommend, argue. It adds a much more human, interactive element to the Internet than five years ago," Stewart said. "Social networking adds the human brainpower to all the information that has been available to us since the onset of the Internet."

What Are Social Networking Tools For?

Conversing: Blogs (short for "Web logs") allow their authors to write about whatever they wish, but they also invite readers to respond. The vast majority of blogs are read by few, but it's a mistake to evaluate them solely on readership. Most are for small audiences—family members, friends, or people who share a narrowly defined interest. For those readers, the value of a blog is in the information it imparts and the opportunity it presents to engage with authors and other readers.

Much the same is true for the most used social networking sites, such as Facebook and MySpace, and for Twitter (the home of super-short, 140-character messages). Media commentators ridicule the vapid content of many public postings, but they're really more akin to the conversations teenagers might have in the mall. They are private conversations that take place in public and have the greatest value to those who are actually part of the conversation.[19]

Sharing: Sites such as Flickr and YouTube allow users to post their own photos and videos for their friends (and anyone else) to see. For most users, they expand, illustrate, or escalate the conversation by adding images and sound to the typed words on the screen. However, others take advantage of the ease of posting, and the extraordinary potential reach of the Internet, to make their creative output available to the world.

Collaborating: Wikipedia works as a different kind of venue for sharing—the sharing of knowledge. Entries can be written and edited by anyone who is motivated to contribute. Of the millions of Wikipedia

(continued)

> entries that make it the world's largest "wiki" (online content that can be edited by readers), there are many that have been enriched by the additions of others. There are also many with little or no value, waiting for contributors with both sufficient knowledge and the willingness to collaborate to make the entries better.
>
> Internal wikis, blogs, and online forums can also be vehicles for collaboration.
>
> *Connecting:* Facebook, MySpace, LinkedIn (a more professionally oriented version of Facebook), Ning, Twitter, and Meetup are all examples of social networking sites that are aimed at making and reinforcing connections among people.

Chapter 8 Key Ideas

- Now more than ever, parents and community members expect to receive information promptly and via the channels they prefer.
- Conversely, parents and community members have the means to disseminate information—or misinformation—quickly and broadly.
- School leaders need to know how parents and staff members communicate with one another and recognize that different audiences may prefer different channels.

Reflections

- What practices has your district used to take advantage of technology in communications?

Practices Your District Could Use to Take Advantage of Technology in Communications

- Create online community forums or blogs to let people ask questions and express their concerns.
- Set up an internal student e-mail system for teacher, parent, and student use.
- Create a flexible online calendar that lets viewers choose the information they will receive (e.g., by school, stakeholder group, or type of event—athletics, fine arts, etc.); allow parents to access the information via computer or smart phone.

9

DEVELOP A STRATEGIC COMMUNICATIONS PLAN

> *The best school communications are planned; the best plans rely on research, analysis, smart implementation, evaluation, and revision.*

Across the country, states, districts and schools are trying to do business differently, to make changes that result in improved student achievement. . . .

People who have been at these kinds of changes for a while have recognized that their efforts to improve school may go nowhere unless they also have a concerted plan for building public support for quality education. And if a reform fails due to lack of public support, the end result is that student achievement doesn't improve.

For those states, schools and districts to be successful, they must focus on changes in policy and practice, but also on strategic communications. Strategic communications is about keeping everyone—starting with the superintendent and school board or state board, whose support is crucial—focused on student achievement, building public support for that achievement, showing what that achievement looks like and demonstrating how improved student achievement benefits everyone.

—Arleen Arnsparger, Adam Kernan-Schloss, Andy Plattner, and Sylvia Soholt[1]

To satisfy your district's communication goals and objectives, your communications must reach the right people and carry the right message, and you must have ways to measure their impact. If not, your district, at best, can't demonstrate that it's using the taxpayers' money wisely and, at worst, is wasting it.

The strategic communications plan is your district's guide to how you will do those three things. It details how the district will employ its scarce resources to communicate effectively and provides yardsticks to gauge how well the district accomplishes the goals it sets for itself.

The communications planning cycle boils down to five steps:

1. assess your district's communications;
2. determine your district's communication goals;
3. implement strategies and tactics designed to achieve your goals;
4. review your progress; and
5. amend the plan as necessary.

ASSESS YOUR DISTRICT'S COMMUNICATIONS

In the corporate and nonprofit sectors, an assessment such as this is referred to as a communications audit. Such audits are frequently performed by someone outside the organization, although they don't necessarily have to be. Organizations use outsiders for their expertise and fresh perspective; for school districts, a communications or public relations firm could do the assessment, as could the National School Public Relations Association (NSPRA). See appendix 5 for an example from our district.

We will describe here how audits work. This way, whether your district engages an outsider or chooses to keep the effort in-house, you'll know what to expect and have a clearer picture of what information and recommendations an audit might yield.

A thorough audit should carefully review your district's communications, including community newsletters, school-based mailings and handouts, teacher newsletters, district forms, websites, e-mails, blogs, SMS postings, building-based signs, bulletin boards, and video message boards. In reviewing these, your auditor should examine what messages are being sent and how well—measured against your district's stated goals and objectives, and against good communication standards. Your auditor should determine whether your communications

- convey specific messages the district wants to disseminate, frequently, using more than one channel;
- address every district goal or objective and to what extent;

- are truthful;
- use channels appropriately;
- explain how interested parties can get more information;
- invite reader or user comments;
- are written clearly, using plain language rather than jargon;
- are written grammatically and proofread before distribution; and
- are presented attractively and make at least some use of photos and graphics.

The audit should make clear who is responsible for handling district communications. Even if your district has a communications person or staff, your administrators, teachers, and support staff all carry out communication responsibilities. After all, they relay information to—and answer questions from—students, parents, families, and others about school matters on a routine basis. And they do more than just answer questions; teachers and support staff frequently create school or classroom newsletters, for example.

A good communications audit should also reveal the district's communications budget, whether communications is a line item in the overall budget or not. For districts that do not have a communications staff, that might be the most important information an audit could uncover.

To get an idea of what your audit might reveal, try this: rough out what your district spends per year on copy paper, toner, and signs. Add outside vendor costs for newsletters, a website, e-mail, automated phone calls, signs, and anything else you think is appropriate. Then ask your school support staff how much of their day they spend answering questions (on the phone or in person) from parents and other community members, preparing and sending information to teachers, creating and sending out mailings and backpack stuffers, and maintaining your website and e-mail system. Prorate their compensation costs based on their answers, and add that to your calculation. Do a back-of-the-envelope estimate of teacher and administrator time devoted to communication, and throw that in, too. We're betting you'll be surprised by the number.

Along with the relatively subjective measures of reviewing existing communication channels and spending, an audit should ask your audiences about how well your communications are working. This typically includes surveys and focus groups. The more comprehensive and rigorous your surveys are, the more useful the results. But basic information you want includes how your audiences feel about the communications they receive; which channels they get their information from now and which channels they would prefer; and what they would like to see improved.

Once this research is done, your auditor can identify the strengths and weaknesses of your district's communications and make recommendations. In the Springfield, Massachusetts, public school system, a K–12 district of twenty-five thousand students, the district's 2009 strategic plan reported the results of an audit:

> The audit determined that the District has been severely hamstrung by a complete lack of a communications operation, taking a haphazard and reactive approach to communicating with the public. The District has made virtually no effort to develop for the news media interesting stories about the school district.
>
> The audit reported that nationally, it is virtually unprecedented for a school district of Springfield's size to function without a Communications Office. It cited Boston as an example. The school district there has six staff members whose primary function is to communicate through the media. In Cambridge, a much smaller district than Springfield, there is one full-time public information officer and a part-time secretary.
>
> In short, the audit established the critical importance for the District to establish a Communications Office and that it become significantly more aggressive in telling its story through the news media and using communications tools and opportunities to more fully engage the public as a whole.[2]

In the Rockwood, Missouri, school district, the audit summarized in its 2009–2010 plan noted the district's strong reputation and general satisfaction with communications reported by internal and external focus groups. However, it also noted some difficulty with internal communication and recommended some changes within the communications department to better address the internal side.[3]

Recommendations such as those cited above become the basis for the next step in the communications plan cycle.

DETERMINE YOUR DISTRICT'S COMMUNICATION GOALS

As the quote at the beginning of this chapter suggests, we are focused not on communication for communication's sake but rather on communication that helps accomplish something larger. Your district's communication goals flow from the overall goals and objectives of the district. Whether your district's goals are broad, such as improving student achievement or enlisting more community support, or specific, such as a referendum campaign or implementation of a new reading curriculum, they stem from your district's intentions and make up the content of your communication.

With the audit and your district goals in hand, your district can craft communications goals that build on the strengths found in the audit, attack the weaknesses, and offer the means for gauging improvement. Suppose, for example, the audit shows that parents of your students believe the district communicates well—but should send out less information on paper and send more electronically. Your district can set a goal to address that. Or suppose the audit finds there are parts of the school community that don't get much communication—non-English speakers, for example. That could lead to a goal to find better communication channels.

The Rockwood communications plan lists each district goal with its related communications goal. So the district goal to "promote, facilitate and enhance parent, student and community involvement in Rockwood School District education programs" is followed by a communications goal to "develop and maintain positive, collaborative relationships with all stakeholders to strengthen support for the Rockwood School District." The district goal to "recruit, attract, develop and retain highly qualified staff to carry out the Rockwood School District's educational programs" is followed by a communications goal to "establish effective employee communication plans to improve internal communication and employee engagement."[4]

IMPLEMENT STRATEGIES TO ACHIEVE YOUR GOALS

Your district's communications strategies should make clear *what* you want to communicate, to *whom*, and *how*. Outlining your strategies should bring specificity into what otherwise can be nebulous and hard to manage. Establishing goals without defining the actions needed to accomplish them can leave administrators wondering where to start, while creating unrealistic expectations for boards and the community. Breaking down the communications process shapes the work into manageable chunks and leads logically to strategies that fit within your district's budget, can be achieved within a predictable time frame, and identify the responsible parties.

Suppose that your district's audit shows your community newsletter is neither well written nor read by many people. You might choose to change the writer or writers, establish new editorial guidelines as to what types of stories belong in the newsletter, promote it vigorously through other channels (such as the website, e-mail, or signs and banners), and schedule a follow-up reader survey after a year's worth of issues to find out whether the newsletter gets more attention and is viewed more favorably. Or your district might decide to scrap the newsletter altogether and devote its limited resources to channels that the audit showed had better reputation or reach. Either strategy can be justified by data and by thinking strategically.

In Elmira, New York, the city school district's 2007–2008 plan directly linked its planned actions to its communications goals. The district objective of a "smooth transition to middle school" led to a communications strategy to "familiarize fifth-graders with the expectations and routines of sixth grade" and a proposed action to "meet with current fifth-graders to discuss sixth grade." The related strategy to "build parent support for revised middle school model" featured proposals to "meet with fifth-grade parents to discuss middle school transition" and to "develop and distribute via Wednesday folders a brochure that explains the sixth-grade model."[5]

REVIEW YOUR PROGRESS

Winning (or losing) a referendum may be the clearest measure of how effectively your district communicates. But you want to know how you're doing well before such a decisive event occurs. The more specifically your district lays out its goals, strategies, and tactics, the easier it will be to monitor progress.

There are a number of measures that can be used to describe the reach and effectiveness of your communications. Simple things can be counted, such as newsletters printed and delivered, website page views, and e-mail subscription requests. Your district can learn something about how effectively activities and opportunities are communicated by the number of people who attend school events or who volunteer in schools.

You can evaluate how well district messages are getting across by conducting follow-up surveys with key audiences and analyzing the results. In addition, you can routinely seek feedback through all available channels and by paying attention to the comments and complaints received. People who take the time to e-mail, post a comment on a forum, write a letter, or call your district can offer case studies for the effectiveness of communications—if respondents seem misinformed or confused about a district initiative, for example, there may be a gap in your information distribution you didn't know was there.

The growth in social networking means that, increasingly, readers expect to be able to comment on or respond to online communications.

Your district may choose to restrict the comments that get published, but both published and nonpublished feedback should be taken into account in your review. Again, the questions and comments may tell you that the district has to explain something in more detail or that you have to work harder to reach certain audiences.

It's important to be clear and realistic about your timetable for reviewing progress. Whether it's quarterly, annually, or longer, everyone involved should know what the evaluation schedule will be. In addition, it should be neither too short (which would not give your plan a fair chance of working) nor too long (which risks leaving failed strategies in place). By creating a communications plan, your district is making a commitment to the community, and you need to uphold every aspect of that commitment.

The plan for the Oklahoma City Public Schools provides an example of connecting goals to measures: "1. Increase awareness by publishing/broadcasting 10 positive stories per month/120 per year about the positive impact of OKCPS education; 2. Improve public perception of schools and the district by 15 percent; 3. Generate engagement and support for the education of OKCPS children measured through increased audience participation and support of OKCPS initiatives by 20 percent."[6]

AMEND THE PLAN BASED ON YOUR REVIEW

Through your district's evaluation, you should be able to understand what constitutes progress for a particular goal. If the goal is on schedule, little may need to be done; if it's not, strategies will need to be examined and revised or perhaps scrapped altogether and new ones put into place.

When your district was setting its overall goals and deciding on strategies, you chose some alternatives and rejected others based on your research, the availability of resources, and the likelihood of success. At review time, you might take another look at those rejected alternatives or look to the experience of other districts to discover fresh ones. The follow-up research and feedback included in your evaluation process also might point to ways strategies can be revised.

Deciding who is responsible for the review is critical. The school board and administrative team are clearly first in line, but the district could benefit if the circle were widened. A committee of board members, administrators, teachers, and community members could take into account the views of outsiders as well as insiders and provide excellent guidance for the communications process.

A recent idea gaining momentum among organizational communicators is a "virtual communications board," which can assist in all aspects of your communications plan. The board consists of a large panel of volunteers from every stakeholder group, who agree to contribute ideas, answer questions, or critique communications on an ad hoc basis.

"The beauty of the virtual communication board is, it never meets," said James Ylisela Jr., president of Chicago-based Duff Media Partners, Inc., and a longtime communications consultant for corporate, nonprofit, and government clients. "That's very appealing to people, because they don't want to go to meetings. They already have too many."

Such a board, Ylisela said, should be composed of a cross-section of an organization's audiences, and the more participants, the better. Board members are expected to respond to periodic e-mails that seek various kinds of feedback. "It might be a question, it might be something that I want you to read, an idea I want you to comment on, or a poll. For example, after an event, I might ask the board 'what was good, what was bad, how can I do it better?'" Ylisela said. "If board members have anything to say, they'll say it; if they don't, they can skip it and wait for the next one. Most people will contribute all the time, but if they're too busy or it's not really their area, we can catch them the next time."

Typically, board members receive a direct e-mail from the person in charge of communications and respond only to the sender. That minimizes e-mails with long strings of replies and helps manage both time and information flow. Besides being an organization's "eyes and ears," the board also provides "a continuous focus group," Ylisela said. While it's not expected to be a statistically representative sample, it's critical that some people from every audience participate. "You don't want only people in one particular audience segment," he said. "If you don't have a good cross-section, you might get a skewed perspective."

Ylisela recommends asking board members to serve a specified period of time and that expectations be made clear. "You want some sort of rotation so that you've got new blood, new perspectives coming in," he said. "Also, you're not asking them to make decisions—you're not seeking edits to newsletter articles, or adding layers to the approval process."

Although he finds e-mails work well, Ylisela notes that the board might also employ wikis or other collaboration-enabling software instead. "It's most important to keep the system very flexible, and that it not be a huge time commitment for anybody," he said. "The goal is to make it instantly worthwhile for the person seeking feedback."[7]

MANAGING COMMUNICATIONS STRATEGICALLY

The basic premise of strategic communications planning is that a district's communications are managed capably. Districts that manage their communications well need to do the following:

- *Be clear.* Make sure communications are logical, well supported, and understandable. Even on complex topics, your messages can be structured simply without being simplistic.
- *Send messages more than once, in more than one way.* Research in communications (and education, for that matter) has long held that audiences don't retain something they see or hear only once. Given that research has also shown that people have different learning styles, it stands to reason that a message will be most effectively delivered if it goes out more than once, in more than one way.
- *Make different channels work together.* Your district's newsletter should promote its website—and vice versa. Use e-mails and SMS not only to broadcast brief, discrete bits of information but also to guide audience members to the places where they can get more detail. Your channels can lead your audiences through the clutter to the information you want them to have.
- *Support the effort from the top.* Regardless of who is in charge of district communications, that person needs support from the superintendent and board. Even in a small district, the amount of information that should be funneled through the communications process is quite large; managing communications well requires the cooperation of every staff member, and that cooperation must be enforced from the top. Closely related to that, your district's chief communicator belongs on the administrative team or cabinet and should be attending their meetings. He or she needs complete, firsthand knowledge of what's going on in the district and should be viewed as a trusted advisor to school leaders.
- *Make it clear who's responsible.* This is true for the same reasons as above, as well as for accountability's sake. Someone has to keep communications issues from falling through the cracks.
- *Encourage cooperation.* Communications within a school district is a *distributed* function—teachers, school secretaries, administrators, and many others share some part of the burden. Without a culture of cooperation, high-quality communications won't happen.

Enforce deadlines. Information that doesn't get out on time reflects badly on the entire district. Part of enhancing communications reach is getting your audiences accustomed to knowing where and when district messages can be seen or heard. Getting it all on schedule, and keeping it there, helps with this process.

Take advantage of opportunities. When a few hundred people are in the school auditorium or gym for the band concert, that's the time to take a moment or two to deliver or reinforce a message. For example, you could use that time to tell parents report cards are coming out soon and to encourage them to talk to their children about them—and have a conversation with their child's teacher if they think it's warranted. Or just reiterate that the district's music program plays an important role in their child's education and in the life of the school and why this is a priority when developing the annual budget.

STRATEGIC COMMUNICATIONS IN A CRISIS

This book is not intended to serve as a crisis communications manual; there are many such resources available to school leaders. However, crises are a time when communications are absolutely critical, and planning ahead gives your district the best chance of communicating well under difficult circumstances. Most districts already have crisis plans in place; you must be sure there is a workable communications component of that crisis plan.

In a crisis, communication both inside and outside the district is vital. Here are a few basic rules for communicating in crises:

- Every district employee should know the plan and know how the district will communicate with them should a crisis arise.
- The crisis plan must identify who is responsible for communicating with authorities, outside agencies, district parents and families, and the public at large.
- With respect to the public, one person should speak for the district, and all employees should know who that person is and how to refer questions. Employees who typically answer outside phone calls must be trained on how to answer calls from emergency responders, worried parents, and the press.
- In commenting to the press and public, the spokesperson's job is to tell everything he or she knows to be true. It's perfectly acceptable

to say, "I don't know," or to refer questions to other authorities. If certain information cannot be released (for legal or privacy reasons, for instance), explain why it can't be released. Avoid saying "no comment."
- It's important for the spokesperson to give updates whenever there is anything new to report. Calm demeanor helps convey an appropriate message even in the most difficult circumstances.
- Whatever has happened, the spokesperson should be sincerely sympathetic. The community will tune out someone who responds by rote, without compassion. A spokesperson should be human, honest, and direct.

Chapter 9 Key Ideas

- Assess your district's communications by conducting an audit.
- Set specific communications goals with benchmarks, strategies, and tactics.
- Review your process regularly and amend the plan based on as much feedback as you can obtain.

Reflections

- What practices has your district used in planning its communications?

Practices Your District Could Use to Plan Its Communications

- Use surveys of the school community and small focus group interviews to provide baseline data before setting communication goals.
- Incorporate regular updates on the communications plan into standard board meetings, board reports, and community communications.

Part III

IT ALL COMES TOGETHER

10

WHAT HAPPENS WHEN YOUR COMMUNICATIONS ARE WORKING

Schools that communicate well are rewarded, because their stakeholders are engaged in their work.

It is important to emphasize in schools, central offices and the community that efforts to improve communication are not apart from the educational agenda, but rather, critical to the success of that agenda. . . . When families and the community are more informed and engaged, they are better prepared to support schools in improving student outcomes.

—Boston Public Schools[1]

The best schools have a vision of what they want to be and work toward realizing it. Communication isn't the vision itself but rather the means to an end—an ever-present, inextricable part of the work that needs to be done. In this example, Richard Weissbourd describes a school that made real an impressive vision of community, morality, and collaboration:

> My children attended a public elementary school that brought both parents and children into a kind of moral community. Interactions with teachers, school events, posters on walls, and communications from our principal worked to connect parents both to one another and to the school. The communications expressed a set of moral commitments—that both parents and children are members of a community and have responsibility for all members of that community; that every student has intellectual and personal contributions to make to the learning of the whole community and that the school has responsibilities to recognize and support these contributions; that school is preparation not only for a career but for many facets of citizenship; that diversity is a high value and that diverse opinions will be

engaged and tested; that students should be taught to identify and address social inequities and injustice. Our parent-teacher conferences often did not focus solely on our own child but on how our child might be helpful to other children in the classroom, as well as on schoolwide concerns and the possible roles parents could play in helping deal with those concerns. Often homework was connected to issues of equity and fairness, and sometimes children were asked to engage parents in this homework. Teachers felt responsibility for all children in the building—not just children in their classroom—and went out of their way to work with children who were marginalized and struggling and to engage the parents of those children. Recently this school was asked to merge with another school with large numbers of children who are academically struggling, a challenge that most schools would be skittish about: this school staff openly embraced this challenge and encouraged parents to embrace it. Because there are trusting, caring relationships between teachers and students at this school, children are also more likely to value what teachers value, including classic virtues such as honesty and courage. At the same time, as the principal observes, "Many parents challenge the larger community to believe in and value each of our students and families. This initiative by families reinforces and sometimes helps lead the school to live up to its values."[2]

Note how communications (between teachers and families, on the walls, and from administrators), values, and trust all play key roles in Weissbourd's story, along with the way the school and its broader community exert a positive influence on one another. It's a powerful story of engagement.

LET YOUR REACH EXCEED YOUR GRASP

We believe top-quality communications help foster important outcomes that comprise key components of any school's vision. To reach this level of communication takes an ambitious vision for the communications plan itself. Communicators in the Rockwood, Missouri, district put together this list of objectives they want their plan to achieve.

Through the implementation of this plan, the following desired behaviors and attitudes are the focus:

Internal Audiences

- Take pride and ownership in the district.
- Keep informed of key issues.

- Work as a high-performing organization whose employees respect and value customer feedback.
- Exhibit district values of caring, integrity, and collaboration.

External Audiences

- Feel involved and engaged in their public schools.
- Exhibit community pride and trust in schools and the district.
- Support the Rockwood School District.[3]

Our own list of the by-products of top-quality communications mirrors both the Weissbourd and Rockwood examples to an extent. We believe such communication fosters the growth of collaboration, helps leaders demonstrate the keeping of expressed commitments, puts values on display, and encourages community participation.

Collaboration

Any district would want its staff members to work in concert; its parents and families to believe they are getting the information they need and have sufficient input into their children's education; and its administrators and teachers to maintain a useful flow of information that goes both ways. These aspirations don't become reality without good communications, both external—about goals and values, or about finances, curriculum, and instruction—and internal—that allows staff members and administrators to be well informed about the district and also promotes their professional development.

Commitments

Implicit in the operation of a school district are promises—the community promises to support the district with its resources, and in turn, school officials promise to educate the community's children. Creation of a communications plan is also a promise: school leaders commit to speaking to—and listening to—the community in a comprehensive, organized fashion. The fact that the district makes the effort to formulate a plan means that school leaders are serious about communicating broadly and well. But to fulfill the promise, the plan must be carried out, and the cycle of research, execution, review, and improvement must be continued.

Many communications plans list principles or guidelines that reflect the district's commitment to its community. The plan for our district specifies that communications should be as follows:

- *Strategic.* Communications will match up with the mission and strategic objectives of the district.
- *Open.* The district will strive to provide clear information to its audiences and to make that information easily accessible and transparent.
- *Honest.* The district will acknowledge mistakes when they occur and provide consistent information about changes, even those that are not immediately embraced by all audiences.
- *Accurate.* The district will work to ensure that information provided to its audiences is complete and factually correct.
- *Timely.* The district will provide accurate and useful information to its audiences when they need it most.
- *Two-way.* Communications will solicit and encourage comments and opinions from the district's audiences, and the district will use that information to inform the community and shape future communication.[4]

Values

The values a district holds show up in its communications in three ways: motivation (the why), content (the what), and execution (the how). If school leaders believe communications are a top priority, they will work hard on the content and execution of those communications. If, on the other hand, school leaders believe other aspects of their jobs have a higher priority than communications, that will be reflected in their actions, too.

For most audiences, the district's values and priorities further show through what school leaders choose to talk about and to put on display. If the district is working to improve student achievement, building safety, or financial practices, those will be written about and discussed. Issues the district doesn't choose to talk about are likely to be viewed as unimportant to the leadership.

District priorities also show through in how its communications are conducted. If school leaders want to reach out to underrepresented segments of the community (such as non-English speakers, senior citizens, or business operators) they will direct communications to them. And if leaders value listening, as well as speaking, their communications will incorporate ways for audiences to talk back. If a district doesn't encourage two-way communication, its leaders appear not to be interested in it—whether that's really true or not.

Engagement

When members of your audience feel welcome in your buildings, when they feel that teachers and administrators care what they think, and when they have evidence that school leaders have the best interests of the community—particularly the community's children—at heart, they feel the sense of ownership and engagement that the Rockwood communicators strive for. Those who feel that sense of ownership volunteer, attend school events, nod affirmatively when you describe your new initiatives, vote for your budgets and tax increases, and give you the benefit of the doubt when there's bad news.

Planned, varied, frequent, substantive communications help people in your community reach that level of engagement. A 2009 document issued by the Harvard Family Research Project and the National Parent Teacher Association (PTA) argues that "robust communication systems" are one of five "promising practices" that promote family engagement with school districts.[5] Specific examples cited in the report included a district in Washington state that conducts workshops for parents to ask questions of teachers and administrators; a Maryland district that uses phone calls, visits to community gathering places, and its Web operation to reach out to families; and a district in Kansas that publishes its calendar and other basic information in three languages and offers streaming video clips on topics such as parenting, curriculum, and how to understand school performance data.

Our standard for community engagement is this: do people in your community talk about *the* schools, or do they talk about *our* schools? Those who talk about *the* schools don't feel the same connection, the same sense of ownership, as do those who talk about *our* schools. Good communication aligns parents with teachers in Weissbourd's "common project together"; gives community members the messages they need to hear in order to feel informed; and lets everyone know they have a role, a voice, and a valued place in the community. It helps create the conditions for learning and for the greatest possible number of people to regard the schools as *ours*.

As we've said repeatedly, communication is critical to everything schools do, but it's only a means to a greater end—that of involving all stakeholders in the serious work of educating children. While this book is more about communication than leadership per se, it's impossible to segregate the two—leaders must be judged in part on their commitment to communicate, their skill in doing so, and the extent to which they can bring their stakeholders together through communication. We'll leave you, then, with this keen observation from the Colorado Association of School Boards:

> Community engagement is on some level a matter of will. Professional staff would rather not suffer the messy inconvenience of outside voices. Community members would rather not take the risks and time of participating in a deliberative process. School boards would rather not listen to public challenges to their judgment or step on the toes of their staffs who wish the board to listen only to them. At its root, therefore, public engagement requires first courage and will from local leadership.[6]

Appendix 1

COMMUNICATION EXAMPLES FROM THE DISTRICT 73½ EDUCATION FUND REFERENDUM IN 2004

In campaigning for a property tax increase in 2004, school officials and the district's volunteer referendum committee crafted communications that addressed different audiences within the school community. Here are some examples:

TO PARENTS

The letter below is one of a series sent from the district to parents, informing them of the district's financial situation and school officials' plans to deal with pressing budget issues. In this example, we outlined the program cuts that we expected to make if the tax vote failed and the cuts we expected to make if the vote passed. We provided this level of detail because we believed parents were primarily interested in how their children's programs would be affected.

January 20, 2004

Dear Parents:

On January 13, 2004, the Board of Education's Finance Committee presented information to the board on proposed budget cuts ranging from $400,000 to $600,000 to be implemented if the March 16 referendum does not pass. If the referendum passes, budget cuts ranging from $100,000 to $180,000 will still need to be made in order to be fiscally responsible.

A description of programs that could be cut follows on the next two pages. There is also a schedule of public meetings to be held during the next two months to provide more information and discussion about budget cuts. We urge all interested residents of the district to attend at least one of these meetings and voice their opinions.

In the last two years the District has already cut more than $400,000. These cuts have affected all three schools as well as district operations. They include reductions in teacher positions, teacher aide positions, secretarial staff, administrative staff, technology, transportation, school supplies and materials, and other programs and services. Additional budget cuts of $400,000 to $600,000 would make it difficult to meet the district's goal to provide a quality program for all students, Pre-K through 8th grade.

Over the years our administrators and staff have developed programs and services to ensure that all students achieve at their highest potential and receive a well-rounded educational program. The district has shown its commitment to providing strong early childhood education as the social and academic foundation necessary for later success in school. At the same time, our district has placed a high priority on delivering a rigorous academic curriculum including expanded opportunities in musical, artistic and physical activities.

Evidence of our success is the Blue Ribbon Award for Excellence in Education that the District received from the U.S. Department of Education in 2002, student achievement measured by state test scores, and progress reports from the high school. In a recent article on state tests (Skokie Review, Jan. 15), District 73½ middle school students outscored all other Skokie schools in state tests in Reading, Writing, Math, Science, and Social Science (www.pioneerlocal.com).

Without increasing revenues, we no longer will have the resources to support our longstanding priorities and provide students with a variety of opportunities to excel. Many programs and services which have contributed to student success are now in jeopardy of being cut.

If the referendum does not pass, the following programs and services will be considered for reduction or elimination:

- *Bus transportation to and from school.* Bus transportation to and from school could be eliminated for all students except for some special education students. Parents would be responsible for getting their children to and from school.
- *The band program, school choirs and musicals.* The award-winning band program—recognized as the finest middle school

band in the state—school choirs, and musicals could be reduced or eliminated. These programs afford students opportunities to appreciate the fine arts and experience them first-hand. Reductions might entail eliminating the part-time percussion instructor position, reducing participation in contests, competitions, and clinics, and curtailing instrument purchases and school performances. Also, band and chorus fees could be increased.
- *Full-day kindergarten.* The full-day kindergarten program could be reduced to a half-day program, with art and music taught by the kindergarten teachers. There would be no lunch program and no formal physical education instruction. The district would not provide extended day child care services. Reduction of full-day kindergarten would likely affect the academic and social readiness of the students in the primary grades and beyond.
- *Increased class sizes at Middleton.* Class sizes in two intermediate grade classrooms could be increased from 20–26 students per class to 25–30, making it harder for teachers to tailor instruction to individuals and small groups. Such "differentiation" within the classroom is critical to many aspects of our current curriculum, particularly in reading.
- *New technology initiatives.* Expenditures would be limited to necessary repairs and equipment replacements. There would be little progress made toward integrating technology into the instructional program, a critical step in educating students in the 21st century.
- *School budgets for purchasing.* For the third year in a row, each building's operating budget would be reduced. This would limit funds to purchase classroom materials and supplies, textbooks, furniture and equipment.
- *Staff development.* There would be fewer opportunities for teachers to attend conferences or work with consultants and curriculum specialists in school, activities which directly affect improvements in curriculum and instruction.
- *Curriculum development.* There would be fewer opportunities for teachers to create, modify, and/or refine instructional teaching units during both the summer and the school year.
- *Middleton ESL/Reading support teacher position.* Support teachers in the areas of reading, ESL and Special Education co-teach in the classrooms and help teachers deliver more individualized instruction for students at all ability levels.
- *Middleton assistant principal position.* Reducing the full-time assistant principal position to a half-time position would

significantly decrease administrative support for students, parents and teachers in the areas of student discipline, curriculum development and special school projects.
- *Middleton reading tutor position.* This would result in less individualized reading instruction for students who read below grade level.
- *One-and-a-half teaching positions at McCracken.* This could affect Experiential Education, Study Skills, Spanish, the Guidance/Counseling program, technology classes, and special classes for 7th and 8th grade students who are two or more grade levels below in reading and math. Overall, 7th and 8th grade class sizes would increase to 28–32.
- *McCracken teacher assistant position.* This could decrease individual and small group assistance to students with special needs (ESL, special education, at-risk).
- *Increased fees for McCracken after-school sports and extracurricular activities.* This would be the second year in a row that fees have increased which could make the cost of participation prohibitive for some students. These activities are part of a well-rounded education and considered essential components of a middle school program.
- *McCracken part-time secretary/substitute teacher position*

If the referendum passes in March 2004, budget cuts ranging from $100,000 to $180,000 will have to be made. Following is a list of possible cuts:

- Pre-K bus transportation
- Decrease in school operating budgets for materials, supplies, textbooks, equipment, furniture, and staff development
- Elimination of a Middleton classroom teacher position by increasing class size in one intermediate grade
- Reduction of the full-time Middleton assistant principal position to a half-time position
- Elimination of a half-time "specials" teacher position in Kindergarten for Art, PE and Music
- Elimination of a part-time teacher assistant position and a part-time secretarial position at McCracken
- Elimination of McCracken's morning band bus and afternoon activity bus

You may share your comments and concerns on budget cuts, questions on the referendum, and suggestions to improve the district's financial situation at upcoming Board meetings: Tuesday,

February 10th and March 9th, 7:00 p.m. at McCracken. Additional evening meetings have been scheduled and parents may attend any of the following regardless of where their children attend: Tuesday, February 3rd, 7:00 p.m., at McCracken; Wednesday, February 18th, at Meyer; Tuesday, February 24th, at Middleton.

It is important that district parents participate in the referendum on March 16, 2004, and exercise their right to vote. If you aren't a registered voter, information on how and where to register is attached. If you have questions, comments, or suggestions please feel free to contact either one of us at _____.

Sincerely,

Vicki Gunther   James A. McGowan
Superintendent   President, Board of Education

* * *

TO STAFF

This document was sent to teachers and support staff members by the volunteer referendum committee. It summarizes the district's financial situation and invites staff members to help with the referendum effort as they may choose, on their own time. Volunteers among the district staff contributed significantly to the success of the campaign.

WHAT, WHY AND HOW

What Is It All About?

- A referendum is the only method available for a school district to increase its revenue from property taxes under the current state-imposed tax cap.
- Property taxes amount to 70 percent of a school district's operating income.
  - State and federal funding bring in another 10–12 percent.
  - The balance comes from student fees, interest income and grants.
- The last referendum was passed in 1990. It has been 14 years since the district has requested a tax rate increase. This means

we have educated an entire generation of school children (K–12) without one.
- Through the referendum campaign, the district reaches out to the community and explains its fiscal standing, requests support for additional revenue, states an amount required to maintain its programs, and lays out the consequences of failing to pass the referendum.
- The referendum is the only viable option left open to the district, which has already cut its budget by more than $400,000 in the last two years. It has reduced staff positions, cut school budgets, sought to save money through joint purchasing agreements, and raised fees.
- Even if the referendum passes, the district will need to reduce spending by another $100,000–$200,000.
- If it fails, the district will have to cut $400,000–600,000 from next year's budget.

What Does This Mean to District Property Tax Payers?

- The referendum seeks a total increase in the tax rate of 75 cents per $100 in equalized assessed property value (EAV).
  - Current maximum is $2.70 per $100 in EAV.
  - New maximum would be $3.45 per $100 in EAV.
- Individual property taxes would increase by about 9.5 percent.
  - If your 2003 property tax bill was $2,000, you would pay an additional $190 in 2004.
  - If your 2003 property tax bill was $3,000, you would pay an additional $285 in 2004.

Why Do We Need a Referendum?

- The district is projecting a $1 million deficit in its Education Fund this year. If current trends continue, the district would run out of money during the 2006–07 school year.
- The findings of an independent auditor and bond counsel agree with the district's projections. If we run out of money, that could lead the state to take over the district.
- The district has made budget cuts and has managed in a fiscally responsible manner. However, expenses go up on average 5 percent per year—health insurance has gone up about 15 percent and the cost of educating at-risk students has approximately doubled in five years. Meanwhile, income

has grown at only about 2 percent per year, due primarily to the limits imposed by the property tax cap.

We also get less support from commercial property owners than in the past. Due to successful tax appeals, the district has been required to refund more than $1 million to commercial property owners since 1999.

- A referendum is the ultimate test of collaboration. In order for the district to properly educate, it needs sufficient funds. In order for the community to thrive, for people to want to move here and contribute to the growth of the community, schools must provide excellent education to students. The referendum is the only way we can preserve the excellent schools we already have.
- Good neighborhood schools are the heart of a strong community.

How Can I Help?

On your own time you can:

- Urge school parents to register to vote. This is critical—the registration deadline is Feb. 17.
  - Join our outreach subcommittee in its voter registration effort.
  - Help make calls—we will have a script for you! Please remember not to use school or district phones when calling parents.
- Urge parents and other school supporters to vote YES on March 16.
- Make a financial contribution to Neighbors for Strong Schools.
- Join our roster of advocates to attend community meetings and speak on behalf of the referendum.
- If you like to walk and talk, we need canvassers. We will need volunteers on weekends in February and March to knock on doors and tell voters why they should vote YES. We are hoping to create two-person teams—a parent and a teacher—to canvass.

Whom Do I Contact to Contribute or Volunteer?

To make a financial contribution, send a check payable to Neighbors for Strong Schools to:

Neighbors for Strong Schools
c/o _____

_____

To help register voters, or to join our roster of speakers, contact one of our outreach subcommittee co-chairs:

To help with canvassing, contact one of our canvass subcommittee co-chairs:

* * *

TO ALUMNI

This letter was mailed to alumni—primarily recent ones—by the volunteer referendum committee. It encourages them to vote and offers help with registering and obtaining absentee ballots, for those who would be away at college on election day. The committee expected young alumni to be inclined to help the district from which they recently graduated.

December 24, 2003

Dear McCracken alumnus,

We hope that you look back fondly at your days at Middleton and McCracken Schools and recognize the value of those early educational experiences in your own growth and development. Like many residents of School District 73½, you most likely feel passionately that good neighborhood schools are the heart of a strong community.

I'm writing to you about voter registration and the March 16, 2004, election. If you have not already done so, you are eligible to register to vote. To make this easier for you, we have set up a time for you to come to McCracken School to register and learn how to cast an absentee ballot if you'll be away at college on March 16. While you're there, please stop by and say hello to Dr. Vicki Gunther, who this year began her new position as Superintendent of District 73½.

Register to Vote
McCracken School
Monday, January 5, from 2 to 5 p.m.

Because you may be home for a brief time over the holiday break, we wanted to be sure to inform you and other District 73½ alumni that one of the questions that will be on the March 16 ballot is a referendum asking for a tax increase in the district's education fund. Like many other Illinois school districts, District 73½ is struggling financially to make ends meet. You can have a direct impact on the life of the district's future students. You can participate in the March election and cast a vote to keep our neighborhood schools strong.

If you'd like to register but can't make it to McCracken on January 5, please call _____ at _____, and she will arrange for a registrar to come to your home at your convenience and help you register. You may also register during regular business hours at the Village Clerk's office at the Skokie Village Hall, 5127 Oakton Street. The deadline for voter registration for the March 16 election is February 17, 2004.

If you've already registered or are planning to register and will be away at college during the election, fill out the form below and return it in the envelope provided. We will mail an absentee ballot application to you when it becomes available.

We have just begun to inform our district residents about the election, so you and your parents will be receiving more detailed information about the needs of our neighborhood schools in the coming weeks. Your help and support are appreciated.

Sincerely,
_____, Chairman
Neighbors for Strong Schools

Yes, I want to help keep my neighborhood schools strong. Please send an absentee ballot application to my college address:
Name: _____
Street Address: _____
City: _____ State: _____ Zip Code: _____

Paid for by Neighbors for Strong Schools
_____, Chairman _____ and _____,
Co-Treasurers

* * *

TO THE SCHOOL COMMUNITY

This example, a summary of the financial situation in an easy-to-understand, question-and-answer format, was prepared by the referendum committee and distributed to registered voters in the district by volunteers going door-to-door.

Appendix 1

FREQUENTLY ASKED QUESTIONS ABOUT THE DISTRICT 73½ REFERENDUM

Why Should I Vote Yes?

- Good neighborhood schools are the heart of a strong community.
- The referendum is the only way we can preserve the excellent schools we already have.
- The district has been run in a fiscally responsible manner, and this referendum is necessary to continue to do so.
- The referendum has to be passed now because any delay will push fund balances too close to zero in the next few years, risking a state takeover of the district.

Why Do We Need a Referendum?

Despite cost cutting, the district's expenses are growing at about 5 percent per year, while income is only increasing at about 2 percent per year. The deficit has been growing yearly, and we're running out of money.

Why Is the District Running Out of Money?

Our expenditures are going up for two major reasons. The cost of educating at-risk and special education students has doubled since 1999. And the district's share of health insurance costs has climbed dramatically—an average of 13 percent a year for the past four years.

At the same time, two major factors are keeping the district's income down. One is the property tax cap, which limits property tax increases to the same growth as the Consumer Price Index (about 2 percent per year recently). The other is property tax appeals by large commercial property owners, which have cost the district more than $1 million in refunds since 1999.

Because of these factors, our fund balances are dropping every year, and we'll run out of money in the 2006–07 school year.

The 2006–07 School Year Is Years Away. Why Do We Need to Pass a Referendum Now?

There are two reasons. One, if a referendum is successful, there's a time lag before the district actually receives new money. If our referendum passes, the district would start seeing new money next fall. If we wait until next year to vote, the new money won't come in before fall 2005.

Two, the district can't let the balances fall all the way to zero before taking action. It's just not fiscally responsible. There are sometimes unscheduled time lags in receiving tax revenues, just as there are sometimes unplanned expenses that need to be taken care of immediately. As a matter of policy, the district keeps at least three months' worth of expenses in its fund balances at all times.

How Will the Referendum Affect Property Taxpayers?

The proposed increase (75 cents per $100 in equalized assessed value, or EAV) would likely raise residential taxpayers' property taxes by about 9.5 percent. District officials and the Cook County clerk's office estimate that it would cost the average homeowner about $300 per year, or about $25 a month (less than the monthly cost of cable TV, for example). For those who have the Senior Citizen Exemption, the increase would be a little less.

Why Can't the District Just Cut Its Budget?

District officials have cut more than $400,000 out of the Education Fund budget during the past two years, and expect to cut at least $100,000 out of next year's, whether the referendum passes or not. They expect to have to cut much more ($400,000 to $600,000) if the referendum fails.

How Have the Cuts Affected the Schools?

So far, the district has been able to maintain its high-quality programs. However, if the referendum fails and the larger cuts have to be made, key educational programs will certainly be affected.

What Will Be Cut?

The board and administration are considering:

- Going from full-day kindergarten to half-day at Meyer School;
- Reducing staff at Middleton and McCracken schools, which would increase class sizes to as many as 30 in some cases;
- Eliminating districtwide bus service (except for special education students);

- Reducing administrative, support and secretarial positions;
- Reducing or eliminating the band, choirs, musicals, sports and other programs.

How Would Those Cuts Affect the Schools?

This district has offered full-day kindergarten for more than 20 years, because the community greatly values early childhood education. Cutting back to half days would affect our young students' readiness for elementary school and beyond.

Increasing class sizes would also have an impact on student achievement. Our teachers and administrators have crafted a curriculum and methods that allow them to address the increasingly varying abilities and needs of their students. The more children there are in a classroom, the more difficult it is to give each student the attention he or she deserves.

Eliminating buses makes families solely responsible for transporting their children to and from school. Reducing classroom and administrative support means vital tasks take longer to get done. Reducing arts and sports programs means students are denied valuable experiences that are closely tied to academic achievement.

I Don't Have Kids in the Schools. Why Should I Help Pay for This?

Consider it an investment. By supporting our schools, you're helping to maintain your overall property values, which have climbed to new highs in recent years. Realtors repeatedly say that buyers value quality schools when shopping for homes, and are willing to pay to live in communities with good schools. By supporting our schools, you're helping to educate the young men and women who will live and work beside you in the future.

Appendix 2

EXAMPLES OF DIFFERENTIATING COMMUNICATIONS

In recent years, much of the discussion about education curricula has revolved around standards. As elsewhere, District 73½ administrators and staff members have worked to apply state standards in their classrooms. In the following two excerpts, we show first how literacy standards for the second grade are described for teachers and then how they are described for parents. The documents show very different levels of detail, but each level is right for its audience.

FOR TEACHERS

Language Arts Power Standards—2nd Grade

Illinois State Goal	State Standards	District Power Standards	Skills and Strategies
#1 Read with understanding and fluency.	A. Apply word analysis and vocabulary skills to comprehend selections.	The student will apply appropriate strategies for decoding and use of context clues to recognize unknown words when reading material. The student will break words into syllables as a decoding strategy.	The student will DECODE TEXT: **Structural** • Understand that every syllable has a vowel. • Recognize and use syllables in words with double consonants

(continued)

Language Arts Power Standards—2nd Grade (*continued*)

Illinois State Goal	State Standards	District Power Standards	Skills and Strategies
		The student will read 150–200 high-frequency words automatically and continue to accumulate high-frequency words working towards automatic knowledge up to the 500 most frequent words. The student will utilize word meanings to build vocabulary.	(ladder) or double vowels (riot). • Form present participle by adding –ing. • Recognize and understand contractions with am (I'm), is (he's), will (I'll), and not (can't). • Recognize and use possessives that add an apostrophe and an s to a singular noun. • Understand the concept of plural nouns and plural forms by adding (s) and (es). • Recognize and form present and past tense verbs by adding (d) and (ed). **Phonetic** • Apply previously taught skills. • Recognize and use all consonant letter sounds and clusters in the beginning, middle, and end of words. • Recognize and use long and short vowel sounds in words.

Illinois State Goal	State Standards	District Power Standards	Skills and Strategies
			• Recognize and use letter combinations that represent long vowel sounds (ai, ay, ee, ea, oa, ow). • Recognize and use phonogram patterns (VC, CVC, CVCe). **Context** • Recognize and use a variety of compound words. • Use known words to read and write unknown words. • Use letters and relationships to sounds to read and write words. • Add, delete, and change letters (in/win, bat/bats), letter clusters (an/plan, cat/catch), and word parts to make new words. • Take apart compound words or join words to make compound words. • Use letter knowledge to monitor reading and spelling accuracy. *(continued)*

Language Arts Power Standards—2nd Grade (*continued*)

Illinois State Goal	*State Standards*	*District Power Standards*	*Skills and Strategies*
			• Use known words and word parts (onsets and rimes) to help in reading and spelling new words (br-ing, cl-ap). • Notice word patterns and categorize high-frequency words to assist in learning them quickly (Word Wall). • Recognize and use synonyms, antonyms, homographs, and homophones • To make past tenses.

Language Arts Power Standards—2nd Grade

Illinois State Goal	State Standards	District Power Standards	Skills and Strategies
#1 Read with understanding and fluency.	A. Apply word analysis and vocabulary skills to comprehend selections. B. Apply reading strategies to improve understanding and fluency. C. Comprehend a broad range of reading materials.	The student will achieve literal understanding by solving words, monitoring and connecting, searching for and using information, and summarizing while reading a text. The student will integrate reading strategies to improve understanding and fluency.	The student will apply COMPREHENSION STRATEGIES: **Connecting** • Bring knowledge from personal experiences to the interpretation of characters and events. • Bring background content knowledge to the understanding of a text before, during, and after reading. • Make connections between the texts and other texts that have been read • Specify the nature of connections (text-to-self, text-to-text, text-to-world). **Predicting** • Use text structure to predict the outcome of a narrative. • Make predictions about the solution to the problem of a story. • Make a wide range of predictions based on personal experiences, content knowledge, and knowledge of similar texts. • Search for and use information to confirm or disconfirm predictions.

(continued)

Language Arts Power Standards—2nd Grade (*continued*)

Illinois State Goal	State Standards	District Power Standards	Skills and Strategies
			• Justify predictions using evidence. • Predict what characters will do based on the traits revealed by the writer. **Summarizing** • Follow and remember a series of events over a longer text in order to understand the ending. • Report episodes in a text in the order they happened. • Summarize ideas from a text and tell how they are related. • Summarize a longer narrative text with multiple episodes. • Identify important ideas in a text and report them in an organized way, either orally or in writing. • Understand the problem of a story and its solution. • Identify the author's purpose, main idea, and supporting details. **Questioning** • Ask questions before, during, and after reading. • Use prior knowledge, information from

Illinois State Goal	State Standards	District Power Standards	Skills and Strategies
			the text, and outside sources to find answers to questions.
• Return to the text to find specific information to find answers to questions.
• Check for understanding and search for information when meaning breaks down.

Inferring
• Infer characters' feelings and motivations through reading their dialogue.
• Demonstrate understanding of characters, using evidence from the text.
• Infer cause and effect in influencing characters' feelings and underlying motives.
• Infer causes of problems or of outcomes in fictions and non-fiction texts.
• Begin to infer the big ideas or message (theme) of a text.
• Identify significant events and tell how they are related to the problem of the story or the solution. |

FOR PARENTS: READING, WRITING, LANGUAGE ARTS

By the end of second grade, students will be able to do the following:

Reading

STRUCTURAL CUES

- Recognize and form contractions with am, is, will and not
- Recognize and use verb endings such as –ing and –ed
- Recognize and use possessive forms of nouns (e.g., cat's)
- Recognize form and use a variety of compound words
- Recognize and use synonyms, antonyms, homographs, and homophones

PHONETIC CUES

- Recognize and use all consonant letter sounds and clusters in words to monitor reading and spelling accuracy
- Recognize and use short and long vowel sounds, and vowel combinations for long vowel sounds (e.g., ai, ay, ee, ea, oa, ow) in words
- Recognize and use patterns in words (e.g., -ack, -ight, -ike)
- Add, delete, and change letters (in/win, bat/bats), letter clusters (an/plan, cat/catch), and word parts to make new words
- Notice word patterns and categorize high-frequency words (word wall words) to assist in learning them quickly

COMPREHENSION

- Understand that enjoyment, information, and comprehension are purposes for reading
- Read fluently and accurately by using appropriate strategies
- Identify important ideas in a text and retell them in an organized way, either orally or in writing
- Identify the author's purpose for writing the text
- Read and compare realistic fiction, simple fantasy, informational texts, poetry, and traditional tales

Appendix 2 137

CONNECTION

- Bring background content knowledge to the interpretation of characters and events
- Make connections across stories that have been read

PREDICTION

- Use text structure to predict the outcome of a narrative (e.g., first, next, then)
- Search for and use information to confirm or adjust predictions
- Justify predictions using evidence

QUESTION

- Return to the text to find specific information that answers questions
- Use prior knowledge, inferences, and outside sources to find answers to questions

INFERENCE

- Use background knowledge and clues from the text to figure out the author's meaning when it is not written in the story

SUMMARIZATION AND MAIN IDEA

- Distinguish the main ideas and supporting details in texts using reading strategies
- Understand the problem of a story and its solution
- Summarize a text briefly including only major ideas
- Identify the order of events in a story

PROCESS TEXT

- Use multiple self-correction strategies (accuracy and meaning) while reading

- Read with high accuracy
- Reflect meaning with voice through pause, stress, and phrasing
- Notice how the layout of pictures and text features affect the way text is read (e.g., bold print, captions)

Writing

IDEAS

- Write several sentences on one topic
- Write complete sentences that make sense

ORGANIZATION

- Write a piece with a clear beginning, middle, and end
- Write in a logical sequence
- Incorporate basic transition words (e.g., first, next, then)
- Write for a variety of purposes (e.g., personal narrative, expository, and author studies)

Appendix 3

CRAFTING THE VISION

Our district's first effort to craft vision and mission statements produced a sizable document that reflected much input from the staff, board, and community. But the document was too long to be memorable or easy to use in the daily life of our schools. The second effort reflected similar values but produced a shorter, more workable set of statements.

THE FIRST TIME AROUND

District 73½ Vision Statements

Following are the District 73½ statements regarding our shared vision for developing lifelong learners, guiding our teaching and learning, and cultivating a district culture to maximize learning. The statements represent the best thinking of District 73½ staff, parents, students, and community members. This "living document" will continue to evolve as we grow and move forward.

OUR VISION STATEMENTS . . .

- are intended to provide a clear sense of direction for our Strategic Plan, which will guide future curricular, extracurricular, financial, and system-wide initiatives
- will help align as well as inspire future actions and decisions
- will apply to all members of our school community—staff, parents, students, members of the Board of Education, administrators, and residents of District 73½.

Vision Statements for Lifelong Learners

It is important for everyone in our school community to acquire the following abilities, characteristics, talents, and qualities.

DISTRICT 73½ LEARNERS—STUDENTS, STAFF, PARENTS, AND COMMUNITY MEMBERS—WILL BE . . .

- Effective communicators who
  - are active and respectful listeners
  - articulate ideas through spoken, written, and artistic means
- Responsible citizens who demonstrate
  - empathy
  - respect for self, others, and the environment
  - honesty and integrity
  - tolerance, patience, and flexibility
  - an appreciation for diversity
  - civic responsibility
  - an awareness of global issues
- Problem solvers who
  - resolve conflicts through good communication, reflection, and compromise
  - develop observational and analytical skills
- Critical thinkers who
  - take intellectual risks
  - actively question
  - apply and synthesize new information
- Well-balanced and caring individuals who
  - maintain a network of healthy relationships
  - identify personal strengths and weaknesses
  - set goals
  - demonstrate physical and emotional wellness
  - appreciate the arts
  - demonstrate a passion for learning
  - cultivate and appreciate humor
- Team players who
  - cooperate in and contribute to group work
  - welcome feedback and provide support to others
  - learn to achieve individual and team goals.

Vision Statements for Teaching and Learning

The following vision statements are intended to guide teaching and learning in the District. They represent conventional wisdom as well as current research on teaching and learning.

DISTRICT 73½ CURRICULUM, INSTRUCTION, ASSESSMENT, AND STAFF DEVELOPMENT PROGRAMS WILL . . .

- Ensure that every learner has the opportunity to reach his/her fullest potential
- Be aligned Pre-K through Grade 8 with State Standards and cooperatively developed in teams within and across grades
- Be implemented, re-evaluated, and revised for continuous improvement
- Reflect best practice based upon research
- Develop concepts and skills to promote higher-order thinking and problem solving
- Balance teacher-directed learning with student-initiated learning and include cooperative groups
- Incorporate technology to enhance learning
- Use flexible grouping to meet learner needs and help every student achieve at his/her highest potential
- Reflect the racial, ethnic, linguistic, and cultural diversity of our students and school community
- Recognize and develop multiple intelligences to meet developmental needs, ability levels, and interests
- Provide experiential learning opportunities and hands-on activities with ample opportunities for practice and application
- Encourage learners to be responsible for their own learning by engaging in self-reflection and self-assessment
- Emphasize connections across subject areas through interdisciplinary study
- Focus on learner results as measured by quantitative and qualitative data
- Provide learners with expanded opportunities for engaging in and appreciating artistic and physical activities
- Integrate the District's vision for Lifelong Learners.

Vision Statements for School Culture

We recognize that learning is influenced by many factors, including the classroom and school environment. To maximize learning for all, we believe the following elements should be valued and reflected in our daily interactions among staff, administrators, students, parents, members of the Board of Education, and the community.

OUR DISTRICT WILL FOSTER A SENSE OF COMMUNITY AND CREATE A CULTURE TO . . .

- Celebrate diversity
- Ensure a safe and secure environment
- Seek opportunities to develop partnerships
- Value traditions
- Encourage participation in decision-making
- Expect clear and direct communication
- Strive for excellence
- Promote positive feelings of self-worth
- Recognize the need for flexibility
- Build relationships
- Nurture collaboration.

THE SECOND TIME AROUND

Skokie School District 73½ Community Meeting
Develop the District's Mission & Vision Statement
Saturday, September 27, 2008

"What Do We Want Our Schools to Be Doing?"

1. SCHOOL LEADERSHIP

District 73½ will employ a professional and knowledgeable staff, who effectively collaborate with the community at large while providing a safe and nurturing school environment.

- Use resources wisely/responsibly (staff)
- Higher/retain highest quality staff (staff)

- Create safe environment (climate)
- Operate within our means (staff)
- Involve all parents (collaborative)
- Adequate resources (staff)
- Lay foundation for adulthood (transition)
- Spirit of fun (climate)
- Healthy students (climate)
- Best instruction practices (staff)
- Support for teachers (staff)
- Transitions (staff)
- Monitor progress (staff)
- Approachable staff (collaboration)

2. LEARNING/KNOWLEDGE (ACADEMICS)

Schools will ensure that all students have the knowledge, skills, and motivation to be problem solvers, and critical, creative, and innovative thinkers.

- Academic support
- Broad-based curriculum
- Love of learning
- Critical thinking
- High achievement/academic standards
- Literate
- Well grounded in fundamentals
- Problem solving
- Opportunity for all learners
- Opportunities beyond core curriculum
- Arts/Foreign Languages that reflect community
- Outside comfort zone
- Good study habits
- Challenge all students
- Time management

3. GOOD JUDGMENT

We want our schools to develop ethical problem solvers who can understand the impact of their actions on themselves, others, and the environment, and work towards making better choices.

- Pride in what you do
- High standards
- Problem solving
- Real-world problems
- Logical thinking
- Honesty/ethics
- Altruistic
- Common sense

4. SOCIAL SKILLS

Our schools need to foster a respectful environment that embraces diverse cultures, opinions, and ideas where students can develop individually, communicate effectively, and work collaboratively to become self-motivated members of society.

- Embracing diversity
- Appreciate other cultures
- Positive SELF development
- Recognize others' good acts
- Respect yourself and others
- Foster character development
- Independent
- Self-motivated
- Teach effective communications

5. RESPONSIBLE CITIZENSHIP (COMMUNITY)

We recognize that the purpose of a public education is to develop good citizens who work toward the common good by understanding their responsibility to be informed citizens and to act upon that knowledge by making positive contributions.

- Volunteer (charitable)
- Graduate good citizens
- Engage with community
- Charitable—giving back

- Appreciate environment
- Common sense

6. INNOVATIVE/CREATIVE

Our schools will foster innovative and creative problem solvers, who can apply their thinking in flexible ways and use their experiences to become positive contributors to the world.

- Critical thinking
- Problem solving
- Foster creativity
- Foster innovation
- Learn from every experience
- Real-world problems
- Think out of the box
- Appreciation of arts

"What Qualities and Abilities Do We Want Our Students to Have by the Time They Graduate?"

1. ACADEMICS

We want our students to possess a passion for learning and demonstrate proficiency in a comprehensive curriculum that will enable them to succeed in a global context.

- To be ready for high school
- Listen well
- Love learning
- Hard working
- Read, write, do math
- Technologically adept
- Know scientific method
- Know grammar, spelling
- Make connections among subject areas
- Speak a second language
- Fiscally responsible

- High expectations
- Understand world

2. CRITICAL THINKING/LEARNING

Our Students will be self-motivated problem solvers who set priorities, achieve high standards, and think independently, logically, and critically.

- Problem solvers
- Independent, logical, critical thinkers
- Have high standards
- Recognize quality work
- Continual improvement
- Set priorities
- Experience to make good choices
- Goal oriented

3. SOCIAL SKILLS (RELATE TO OTHERS)

We want our students to be: thoughtful, responsible, and collaborative citizens, who appreciate themselves and others, and adapt to and improve the changing world around them.

- Kind/compassionate
- Respectful
- Thoughtful
- Responsible
- Communicate well
- Tolerant
- Flexible (adaptable)
- Empathetic
- Other-centered
- Know actions have consequences
- Work well with others/collaborate
- Make connections between school/out of school
- Be good leaders, followers; know when to lead—when to follow
- Appreciate (seek out) diversity
- Knowledge of the world—understand place _____

- Appreciate what a great District this is
- Realize that adults care for them
- Appreciate "The Village" is raising them (PTA/Foundation)

4. SELF-AWARENESS

Be confident, self-motivated learners who have high expectations and through self-advocacy and perseverance achieve their goals.

- Self-motivated
- Goal oriented—not afraid to fail
- High expectations
- Be observant
- Advocate for selves
- Confident/optimistic
- Emotionally self-regulating
- Curious
- Vision for future/foundation to achieve it
- Realistic
- Appreciate what you have
- Act the same everywhere
- Sense of culture/artistic values
- Recognize and be a role model
- Self-esteem

These statements were winnowed down to four guiding principles:

- Our schools will support and inspire our students
- Our students will be critical thinkers and creative problem solvers
- Our community will demonstrate integrity and respect
- Our graduates will help make the world a better place

Appendix 4

TEACHER-FAMILY COMMUNICATIONS

District administrators worked with Complete Communications, Inc., to create this presentation for teachers on family communications. Because teachers and administrators set a districtwide goal of improving student assessments, the focus of the presentation was to help teachers communicate their assessments better, particularly in conferences. After review and discussion, teachers broke up into groups of three and role-played the three scenarios at the end of the slides—each one played the role of teacher in one, parent in another, and observer in a third.

TEACHER-FAMILY COMMUNICATIONS
MIDDLETON SCHOOL
MARCH 23, 2010

The Context for This Session

- Formal conferences and informal interactions
- Ongoing work about formative assessments

What Teachers Can Do

- Encourage parents and families to visit www.sd735.org, school, grade-level and teacher websites
- Reinforce guiding principles:
  - Our schools will support and inspire our students
  - Our students will be critical thinkers and creative problem solvers

Appendix 4

- Our community will demonstrate integrity and respect
- Our graduates will help make the world a better place

What Parents Want from Conferences

- To believe you know their child
- Concrete examples
- To know there is a plan to help their child make progress
- How they can help

Format for Conferences

- Make a human connection first
- Summarize the child's strengths
- Summarize opportunities for growth
- Lay out the plan
- Tell parents how they can help
- Let parents respond
- Answer their questions

Suggestions for Parents

- What can they do to support strong students?
- What can they do to support weak students?

Parent Comments and Questions

- Be patient
- Don't take challenging questions personally
- Make sure they know who to call with questions or concerns
  - Teacher
  - Principal
  - Superintendent

How to Talk About Assessment

- Help parents understand targets, standards, and assessments
  - What goal is the student working toward?
  - Why are certain assessments used? What do they tell us?

- Explain how assessment helps students
- Explain how parents can help

Handling Difficult Conversations

- Prepare
- Watch what you say
  - Avoid value-laden terms (stupid, lazy)
  - Don't take out difficult parent interactions on the student
- Try to keep things calm

Your Rights

- You can call for an administrator to join you
- You can end the meeting
  - Ask parent to leave
  - Set up a subsequent meeting with you and an administrator
- You can leave the room
- You can call police if you feel threatened

Scenario 1—Conference

1. Teacher
2. Defensive parent of a student who is weak academically, popular, and sometimes disruptive
3. Observer

Scenario 2—Conference

1. Observer
2. Teacher
3. Uncomfortable parent of a student who is very strong academically, shy, and awkward

Scenario 3—Conversation

1. Teacher who has observed a student bullying others
2. Angry parent of student
3. Observer

Appendix 5

COMMUNICATIONS AUDIT

In 2008–2009, our district worked with Complete Communications, Inc., to develop its first communications plan. These two excerpts summarize the findings of the communications audit.

2. OVERVIEW

There are many indicators that the district is doing an adequate job of communicating. No major issues publicly divide the community, nor are there public allegations of information withholding. High percentages of respondents to our online surveys of community residents and staff said the district communicates at least fairly well.

But at the same time, there are serious issues to address. The surveys, board and administrative feedback, and focus groups all indicate that the district's electronic communications need to improve. Most survey respondents want the district's Web operation to be a main source of information, and they want information available by e-mail. In addition, the opportunities for richer, deeper communication offered by multimedia content and the use of social networking tools are increasing by the day.

The district can improve in other communication areas as well. Print communications can be better planned and executed, and there can be more planning and training in often-overlooked communications areas such as the staff's interactions with parents or guardians and other community members. As part of its adoption of the professional learning community (PLC) model, the district has established clear messages that it wants to convey to all its audiences; those messages need to be delivered through all the district's available means of communication.

Communication is no trivial matter. We estimate that the district spends about $550,000 a year on communications. Public school districts are forced to watch their expenses very carefully; this area is no exception, and the district should plan and evaluate to ensure that it gets the most for its money.

For District 73½, the communications story isn't about fixing a broken system; it's about seizing opportunities to make a good situation better.

5. RESEARCH SUMMARY

The research Complete Communications conducted involved a review of more than 40 printed pieces, the district and individual school websites, interviews with administrators and support staff, online surveys of community members and teachers, and focus group sessions with parents and community members. An attempt to run a focus group made up of ELL parents failed, but did result in an in-depth interview with one parent. A list of pieces analyzed, raw survey results and lists of focus group participants are included in an appendix to this document.

Key findings that are reflected in this plan include:

a. Print pieces were inconsistent in look and feel, design quality and alignment with district goals. Overall, they met the minimum in terms of specific information provided, but many could have accomplished more.

b. The websites were also inconsistent in look and feel, and were rife with outdated items. In particular, navigation was inconsistent and some focus group members said it was difficult to find specific information.

c. Most of the 112 community survey respondents said the district communicated very well (39 percent) or fairly well (38 percent). Fewer than one-tenth rated the district's communication as somewhat poor (6 percent) or very poor (3 percent). The percentages were roughly the same whether respondents currently have children in a district school or not. The overwhelming majority of district employees agreed—37 percent said the district communicates very well and 52 percent said it communicates fairly well.

d. Websites were cited most often as one of the best ways for the district to communicate with the community in both the community survey (53 percent) and the staff survey (69 percent). A majority of community respondents (51 percent) also cited e-mail as one of the best means of communication. Parents in the focus group sessions agreed strongly with the use of e-mail, with many voicing the opinion that they receive "too much paper."

e. Those community respondents who said a language besides English is spoken in their homes were not very interested in receiving translated communications from the district. Of the 39 respondents who so identified themselves, 29 said they did NOT want translated information. On the other hand, when staff members were asked whether the district should provide translated information to the community, 79 percent said yes—a strong indication that those who work most closely with the district's families see a need for this.

f. Segments of the community that the district finds hardest to reach were, not surprisingly, least well represented in the surveys and focus groups. These include residents for whom English is not their first language, and district business operators. More research needs to be done to draw definitive conclusions about these audiences.

NOTES

INTRODUCTION

1. Twin Rivers Unified School District, "2008–2009 Communications Plan," North Highlands, CA, 2008, 1.
2. Quoted in Frank Deford, "The Rabbit Hunter," *Sports Illustrated*, January 26, 1981.
3. Roland Barth, foreword to *Leading and Learning*, by Fred Steven Brill (Portland, ME: Stenhouse, 2008), ix.

CHAPTER 1: THE PUBLIC HAS A RIGHT TO KNOW

1. 1977 N.Y. Laws, ch. 933. This is one of many examples of statements of philosophy or purpose in open government laws in various states. For a compilation of such laws in the fifty states and District of Columbia, visit the Reporters Committee for Freedom of the Press Open Government Guide at www.rcfp.org/ogg.
2. David Kidwell and Bob Goldsborough, "Wheaton Warrenville School Board to Release Records, Illinois Supreme Court," *Chicago Tribune*, May 22, 2009.
3. Quoted in Scott LaFee, "Transparency," *School Administrator* 66, no. 1 (January 2009): 11–12.
4. Megan Tschannen-Moran, *Trust Matters: Leadership for Successful Schools* (San Francisco: Jossey-Bass, 2004), 25.
5. Douglas J. Fiore, *School-Community Relations* (Larchmont, NY: Eye on Education, 2002), 89.
6. Lisa Black, "Antioch District Decides against Book Ban," *Chicago Tribune*, June 23, 2009.
7. Maura J. Casey, "So Is That Like an A?" *New York Times*, February 14, 2008.
8. Lake Mills Community School, physics class Web page, Lake Mills, IA, at www.lake-mills.k12.ia.us/hs/sci/phy-e4.html (accessed October 8, 2010).

CHAPTER 2: SCHOOL DISTRICTS NEED TO ENGENDER TRUST

1. Megan Tschannen-Moran, *Trust Matters: Leadership for Successful Schools* (San Francisco: Jossey-Bass, 2004), 15.
2. Deborah Meier, *In Schools We Trust* (Boston: Beacon, 2002), 3.
3. Anthony Bryk and Barbara Schneider, *Trust in Schools: A Core Resource for Improvement* (New York: Russell Sage Foundation, 2002), 5.
4. Stephen R. Covey, *The 7 Habits of Highly Effective People: Powerful Lessons in Personal Change* (New York: Free Press, 1989), 188.
5. Stephen R. Covey, *The 8th Habit: From Effectiveness to Greatness* (New York: Free Press, 2004), 162. For a thought-provoking list of ten ways to make deposits into your trust account, see "Moral Authority and the Speed of Trust" on page 165 of the *8th Habit*. Covey provides a chart of the ten key deposits and withdrawals, the sacrifices required, and the internalized principles involved.
6. Tschannen-Moran, *Trust Matters*.
7. Julia Haley, former school superintendent in Northbrook, IL, personal communication, March 22, 2010.
8. William Glasser, *The Control Theory Manager* (New York: HarperCollins, 1994), 19.
9. William Glasser, *The Quality School: Managing Students without Coercion*, 2nd ed. (New York: Harper Perennial, 1992).
10. Linda Hanson, search consultant and former superintendent in Highland Park, IL, personal communication, October 21, 2009.
11. Tschannen-Moran, *Trust Matters*, 26.
12. Peter Spiegel, "Report: Air Force Flubbed Missile Checks," *Los Angeles Times*, October 20, 2007.
13. Dick Streedain, university professor, consultant, and former principal of Hubbard Woods Elementary School, Winnetka, IL, personal communication, August 22, 2009.
14. Dick Streedain, personal communication, March 5, 2010.
15. Margaret Wheatley, "Goodbye, Command and Control," *Leader to Leader* (July 1997).
16. Ed Rafferty, superintendent of Community Consolidated School District 54, Schaumburg, IL, personal communication, November 24, 2009.
17. James P. Spillane and John B. Diamond, *Distributive Leadership in Practice* (New York: Teachers College Press, 2007).
18. Stephen M. R. Covey, with Rebecca R. Merrill, *The Speed of Trust: The One Thing That Changes Everything* (New York: Free Press, 2006), 223.
19. Covey and Merrill, *Speed of Trust*, 229.
20. Stacey Childress, "Six Lessons for Pursuing Excellence and Equity at Scale," *Phi Delta Kappan* 91, no. 3 (November 2009): 17.

21. Diane E. Reed, Allison J. Armstrong, and Renee A. Williams, "Laptops and Communication Lessons," *School Administrator* 62, no. 7 (August 2005), at www.aasa.org/SchoolAdministratorArticle.aspx?id=8468 (accessed August 3, 2010).

22. Reed, Armstrong, and Williams, "Laptops and Communication Lessons."

23. Fred Brill, superintendent of Lafayette School District, Lafayette, CA, personal communication, February 7, 2010.

CHAPTER 3: SCHOOL DISTRICTS NEED TO ADVOCATE FOR THEMSELVES

1. Kitty Porterfield and Meg Carnes, *Why School Communication Matters: Strategies from PR Professionals* (Lanham, MD: Rowman & Littlefield Education, 2008), 87.

2. See John Hechinger and Suzanne Sataline, "For More Mayors, School Takeovers Are a No-Brainer," *Wall Street Journal*, March 12, 2009.

3. See Greg Burns, "Education Secretary Arne Duncan Counting on Business Leaders to Help Push through School Reforms," *Chicago Tribune*, July 6, 2009.

4. See, for example, Lynn Moore, "Superintendents Taking Case to People—through Videotape (Videos)," *Muskegon (Michigan) News*, January 24, 2010.

5. William J. Bushaw and John A. McNee, "Americans Speak Out: Are Educators and Policy Makers Listening? The 41st Annual Phi Delta Kappa/Gallup Poll of the Public's Attitudes toward the Public Schools," *Phi Delta Kappan* 91, no. 1 (September 2009): 8–23.

6. Griff Powell, former school superintendent in Illinois and New York, personal communication, December 28, 2009.

7. Susan Lucia Annunzio, *Contagious Success: Spreading High Performance throughout Your Organization* (New York: Penguin, 2004), 88–90.

8. Linda Tafel, professor, National-Louis University, personal communication, October 10, 2009.

9. Section 204 of the Child Nutrition and WIC Reauthorization Act of 2004.

10. Trinette Marquis, director of communications, Twin Rivers Unified School District, North Highlands, CA, personal communication, December 24, 2009.

11. Marquis, personal communication.

12. Marquis, personal communication.

13. Frank Porter, superintendent, Twin Rivers Unified School District, North Highlands, CA, personal communication, December 24, 2009.

14. Bill Berg, "Mind over Media," Media Educational Services, Addison, IL, 1990.

15. Ed Rafferty, personal communication, November 24, 2009.

16. Porterfield and Carnes, *Why School Communication Matters*, 35.

CHAPTER 4: KNOW WHO'S LISTENING AND HOW TO REACH THEM

1. Jim Kouzes and Barry Posner, "The Five Practices of Exemplary Leadership," in *The Jossey-Bass Reader on Educational Leadership*, 2nd ed. (San Francisco: Wiley, 2007), 66.
2. Richard J. Stiggins, Judith A. Arter, Jan Chappuis, and Stephen Chappuis, *Classroom Assessment for Student Learning* (Portland, OR: Assessment Training Institute, 2004), 295.
3. Boston Public Schools, "Strategic Communications," Boston, 2006.
4. Alum Rock Union Elementary School District, "Strategic Communications Plan," San Jose, CA, September 2009, at www.arusd.org/202510616123950867/lib/202510616123950867/STRATEGIC_COMMUNICATIONS_PLAN2009-2010.pdf (accessed March 22, 2010).
5. Twin Rivers Unified School District, "2008–2009 Communications Plan," North Highlands, CA, 2008.
6. Griff Powell, personal communication, November 23, 2009.
7. Elmira City School District, "Communication Plan 2007–08," Elmira, NY, at www.elmiracityschools.com/uploadeddocs/07.08.communication.plan.pdf (accessed March 22, 2010).
8. Sarmad Ali, "With Online Services, Foreign Texts Can Get Lost in Translation," *Wall Street Journal*, December 20, 2007.
9. Peel School District, "Peel District School Board Micro-Web Sites in 25 Languages," at www.iabc.com/education/pdf/Link_CS4_Slides.pdf (accessed January 27, 2010).
10. International Association of Business Communicators, "Gold Quill Awards: The Business Issue Award," at www.iabc.com/awards/gq/businessissueaward.htm (accessed January 27, 2010).
11. WebContent.gov, "Ways to Analyze Your Audience," at www.usa.gov/webcontent/improving/evaluating/audience.shtml (accessed March 22, 2010). WebContent.gov is an official website of the U.S. government, managed by the Federal Web Managers Council and sponsored by the General Services Administration's Office of Citizen Services and USA.gov.
12. Edward Tufte is a renowned authority on the visual presentation of data. More information on his work can be found at www.edwardtufte.com/tufte.
13. A district that uses e-mail blasts effectively is Rockford Public Schools in northern Illinois. To see how it works, sign up online at http://rps205.com/emaillist.
14. Twin Rivers Unified School District, "2008–2009 Communications Plan."
15. Twin Rivers Unified School District, "2008–2009 Communications Plan."
16. Beaverton (Oregon) School District home page, at www.beaverton.k12.or.us/home (accessed October 11, 2010).

CHAPTER 5: ALIGN COMMUNICATIONS WITH DISTRICT GOALS AND VALUES

1. Douglas Reeves, *The Daily Disciplines of Leadership: How to Improve Student Achievement, Staff Motivation, and Personal Organization* (San Francisco: Jossey-Bass, 2002), 91.

2. Rebecca Harris, "I Have Somewhere to Go," *Catalyst Chicago* (January 2010), at www.catalyst-chicago.org/news/index.php?item=2620&cat=32 (accessed May 27, 2010).

3. Richard Weissbourd, *The Parents We Mean to Be: How Well-Intentioned Adults Undermine Children's Moral and Emotional Development* (Boston: Houghton Mifflin Harcourt, 2009), 115–16.

4. Sylvia Soholt, "Public Engagement: Lessons from the Front," *Educational Leadership* 56, no. 2 (October 1998): 22–23.

5. Robert S. Kaplan and Dylan N. Miyake, "The Balanced Scorecard," *School Administrator* 67, no. 2 (February 2010): 12. For an example of Atlanta Public Schools' balanced scorecard, go to www.atlantapublicschools.us/18611010817914830/lib/18611010817914830/APS_Balanced_Scorecard-2009-10.pdf (accessed October 11, 2010).

6. Kaplan and Miyake, "The Balanced Scorecard."

7. Charlotte-Mecklenburg (NC) Schools, school district dashboard data samples, at http://pmd.cms.k12.nc.us/Strategic%20Goals/Goal%20I%20-%20High%20Academic%20Achievement/Overall.aspx (accessed July 15, 2010).

8. Robert M. Avossa, chief accountability officer, Charlotte-Mecklenburg Schools, personal communication, May 26, 2010.

9. Sally Leonard, "Opportunities Lost: A Few Pointers on PR from an Educational Marketer," *Education Week* 23, no. 11 (November 12, 2003): 29–30.

10. Roland Barth, "A Personal Vision of Schooling," *Phi Delta Kappan* 70, no. 7 (March 1990): 513–14.

11. Fred Brill, personal communication, February 7, 2010.

12. Carlos Azcoitia, former deputy superintendent and principal, Chicago Public Schools, personal communication, October 7, 2009.

13. Dick Streedain, personal communication, August 22, 2009.

14. Adam Kernan-Schloss and Andy Plattner, "Talking to the Public About Public Schools," *Educational Leadership* 56, no. 2 (October 1998): 22.

15. Frank Porter, personal communication, December 24, 2009.

16. Alica Diebel, "Public Engagement in Five Colorado School Communities: A Report from the Colorado Association of School Boards," *Connections 2007* (annual newsletter of the Kettering Foundation), at www.kettering.org/foundation_programs/public_education/public_engagement_in_five_colorado_school_communities (accessed June 2, 2010).

17. Robert J. Marzano, Timothy Waters, and Brian A. McNulty, *School Leadership that Works: From Research to Results* (Alexandria, VA: ASCD, 2005), 46.

18. Milbrey W. McLaughlin and Joan E. Talbert, *Building School-Based Teacher Learning Communities: Professional Strategies to Improve Student Achievement* (New York: Teachers College Press, 2006), 33. The authors attribute the phrase "a community of explanation" to Donald Freeman, *Towards a Descriptive Theory of Teacher Learning and Change* (Brattleboro, VT: Center for Teacher Education, Training and Research, School for International Training, 1999).

19. More information on protocols can be obtained from the National School Reform Faculty at www.nsrfharmony.org/protocols.html and from Teachers College Press at www.tcpress.com/pdfs/mcdonaldprot.pdf. Mid-continent Research for Education and Learning (McREL) has published a report featuring a rubric that illustrates the connection between communication practices and success in creating a PLC; see "Sustaining School Improvement: Professional Learning Community" (2003) at www.plcwashington.org/introduction/resources/MCREL-rubric.pdf (accessed October 12, 2010). Other useful PLC rubrics can be found in Richard DuFour, Rebecca DuFour, Robert Eaker, and Thomas Many, *Learning by Doing: A Handbook for Professional Learning Communities at Work* (Bloomington, IN: Solution Tree, 2006).

20. Tod Lending and David Mrazek, *The Principal Story* (Chicago: Ethno Pictures, Nomadic Pictures, Wallace Foundation, 2009). This documentary film, first shown on PBS in fall 2009, highlights the challenges school leaders face in raising student achievement in low-performing schools.

21. Stephen R. Covey, *The 8th Habit: From Effectiveness to Greatness* (New York: Free Press, 2004), 174.

CHAPTER 6: SHOW, DON'T TELL

1. Jennifer Laszlo Mizrahi and Talton Gibson, "Winning Advocacy," *School Administrator* 61, no. 3 (March 2004): 11.

2. Roland Barth, foreword to *Leading and Learning*, by Fred Steven Brill (Portland, ME: Stenhouse, 2008), x.

3. Marianne Dainton and Elaine D. Zelley, *Applying Communication Theory for Professional Life* (Thousand Oaks, CA: Sage, 2005).

4. Cited in Douglas Reeves, "Making Strategic Planning Work," *Educational Leadership* 65, no. 4 (December 2007/January 2008): 86–87. The Freeport "plan on a page" can be viewed online at www.freeportschooldistrict.com/fsd145/lib/fsd145/0910_Plan_on_a_Page.pdf.

5. For information about "The Daily Five," see www.thedailycafe.com/public/department38.cfm.

6. Skokie (Illinois) School District 73½, "Community Digest," fall 2009, at www.sd735.org/education/components/scrapbook/default.php?sectiondetailid=2647& (accessed October 12, 2010).

CHAPTER 7: CULTIVATE CREDIBILITY

1. Irene Navis, "The Importance of Credibility," American Society for Public Administration blog, August 4, 2009, http://aspanational.wordpress.com/2009/08/04/the-importance-of-credibility (accessed July 18, 2010).

2. Stephen M. R. Covey with Rebecca R. Merrill, *The Speed of Trust: The One Thing That Changes Everything* (New York: Free Press, 2006), 58.

3. Covey and Merrill, *Speed of Trust*, 58. In *The Speed of Trust*, Covey lists thirteen behaviors characteristic of trusted leaders: talk straight; demonstrate respect; create transparency; right wrongs; show loyalty; deliver results; get better; confront reality; clarify expectations; practice accountability; listen first; keep commitments; and extend trust.

4. Griff Powell, personal communication, November 23, 2009.

5. Colorado Association of School Boards, "Public Engagement in Five Colorado School Communities: Report to the Kettering Foundation," Denver, July 15, 2003, 6–7.

6. Reported in the *Skokie Review* (Illinois), "Stingy Tax Caps Impact 73.5 Levy," November 16, 2009.

7. Scott LaFee, "Transparency," *School Administrator* 66, no. 1 (January 2009): 12. In the article, LaFee wrote about four school districts that received the NSPRA Gold Medallion Award honoring their public relations programs.

8. LaFee, "Transparency," 12.

9. Bill Berg, "Mind over Media," Media Educational Services, Addison, IL, 1990.

10. *Wall Street Journal*, "Gulf News Urges Reporters to Tone Down Dubai Coverage," December 24, 2009.

11. Ed Rafferty, personal communication, November 24, 2009.

12. LaFee, "Transparency," 14.

13. In a commentary discussing President Barack Obama's handling of the 2010 oil spill in the Gulf of Mexico, *New York Times* writer Peter Baker discussed how commonly passive voice is used during crises: "Admitting fault, after all, is not a common presidential habit, and happens only under great duress. The passive voice has been a favorite technique. President George [H. W.] Bush said 'mistakes were made' during Iran-contra. President Bill Clinton said 'mistakes were made' during campaign finance scandals. And President George W. Bush said 'mistakes were made' during the firing of federal prosecutors." See Peter Baker, "Responding to Spill, Obama Mixes Regret with Resolve," *New York Times*, May 27, 2010.

CHAPTER 8: TAKE ADVANTAGE OF TECHNOLOGY

1. Clay Shirky, *Here Comes Everybody: The Power of Organizing without Organizations* (New York: Penguin, 2008), 23.

2. Jeffrey S. Arnett, personal communication, June 8, 2010.

3. Shirky, *Here Comes Everybody*, 18.

4. Jennifer Mendelsohn, "Honey, Don't Bother Mommy. I'm Too Busy Building My Brand," *New York Times*, March 12, 2010.

5. Shirky, *Here Comes Everybody*. Shirky cites multiple examples of such groups coming together by means of the Internet and social networking.

6. Brent LaMaire, "Governments Find Twitter Effective at Combatting Rumors: Agencies, Pols, States Adopt New Form of Rapid Response," June 21, 2010, at http://ohmygov.com/blogs/general_news/archive/2010/06/21/governments-find-twitter-effective-at-combatting-rumors.aspx (accessed October 13, 2010).

7. Kevin Butler, "Tweeting Your Own Horn," *District Administration* (February 2010), at www.districtadministration.com/viewarticle.aspx?articleid=2281 (accessed March 23, 2010).

8. Trent Toone, "Creativity, Imagination Churned Out through Teachers' 'Machine,'" *Ogden Standard-Examiner* (Utah), December 23, 2009.

9. Jim Warren, "Harrison School District Gets Award," *Lexington Herald-Leader* (Kentucky), December 5, 2009.

10. Grunwald Associates LLC, in cooperation with the National School Boards Association, "Creating and Connecting/Research and Guidelines on Online Social—and Educational—Networking," National School Boards Association, Alexandria, VA, July 2007, at www.nsba.org/SecondaryMenu/TLN/CreatingandConnecting.aspx (accessed August 5, 2010).

11. Georgia Garvey, "Evanston Goes Web Route for Budget Help," *Chicago Tribune*, December 30, 2009.

12. See City of Evanston, "FY2011 Budget," at www.cityofevanston.org/budget (accessed October 13, 2010).

13. See Shenendehowa Central Schools, "Heard It through the Grapevine," at www.shenet.org/grapevine (accessed October 13, 2010).

14. Kelly M. DeFeciani, public information officer, Shenendehowa Central Schools, Saratoga County, NY, personal communication, February 3, 2010.

15. L. Oliver Robinson, "Combating the Rumor Mill through a Grapevine," *School Administrator* 67, no. 1 (January 2010), at www.aasa.org/SchoolAdministratorArticle.aspx?id=11048 (accessed March 23, 2010).

16. DeFeciani, personal communication.

17. See Etienne Wenger, *Communities of Practice: Learning, Meaning and Identity* (New York: Cambridge University Press, 1998).

18. Nancy Stewart, teacher, Avoca School District 37, Wilmette, IL, personal communication, February 2, 2010.

19. To see how a Seattle private school uses Twitter, go to www.youtube.com/watch?v=0N6hs0YN7Yg (accessed October 13, 2010).

CHAPTER 9: DEVELOP A STRATEGIC COMMUNICATIONS PLAN

1. Arleen Arnsparger, Adam Kernan-Schloss, Andy Plattner, and Sylvia Soholt, "Building Community Support for Schools: A Practical Guide to Strategic Communications," Education Commission of the States, Denver, June 1997, 3, at www.eric.ed.gov/PDFS/ED410606.pdf (accessed July 8, 2010).
2. Springfield Public Schools, "Strategic Communications Plan," Springfield Public Schools, Springfield, MA, March 2009, at www.sps.springfield.ma.us/deptsites/communications/content/SPSStrategicCommunicationsPlan.pdf (accessed August 9, 2010).
3. Rockwood School District, "Comprehensive Communications Plan 2009–2010." Rockwood Communications, Wildwood, MO, 2009, at www.rockwood.k12.mo.us/communications/Downloads/Comprehensive%20Communications%20Plan%202009-2010.pdf (accessed February 26, 2010).
4. Rockwood School District, "Comprehensive Communications Plan 2009–2010."
5. Elmira City School District, "Communication Plan 2007–08," Elmira, NY, at www.elmiracityschools.com/uploadeddocs/07.08.communication.plan.pdf (accessed March 22, 2010).
6. Kathleen Kennedy, "Oklahoma City Public Schools: Communications Strategic Plan 2008–2009," at www.okcps.k12.ok.us/Communications (accessed February 25, 2010),11.
7. James P. Ylisela Jr., communications consultant, personal communication, June, 2010.

CHAPTER 10: WHAT HAPPENS WHEN YOUR COMMUNICATIONS ARE WORKING

1. Boston Public Schools, "Strategic Communications," Boston, 2006, 2.
2. Richard Weissbourd, *The Parents We Mean to Be: How Well-Intentioned Adults Undermine Children's Moral and Emotional Development* (Boston: Houghton Mifflin Harcourt, 2009), 124–25.
3. Rockwood School District, "Comprehensive Communications Plan 2009–2010," Rockwood Communications, Wildwood, MO, 2009, at www.rockwood.k12.mo.us/communications/Downloads/Comprehensive%20Communications%20Plan%202009-2010.pdf (accessed February 26, 2010).
4. District 73½, internal communications plan memo, March 2009.

5. Helen Westmoreland, Heidi M. Rosenberg, M. Elena Lopez, and Heather Weiss, "Seeing Is Believing: Promising Practices for How School Districts Promote Family Engagement," Harvard Family Research Project and National Parent Teacher Association (PTA), issue brief, July 2009, at http://pta.org/Issue_Brief-SeeingisBelieving.pdf (accessed June 3, 2010).

6. Colorado Association of School Boards, "Public Engagement in Five Colorado School Communities: Report to the Kettering Foundation," Denver, July 15, 2003, 23.

BIBLIOGRAPHY

Ali, Sarmad. "With Online Services, Foreign Texts Can Get Lost in Translation." *Wall Street Journal*, December 20, 2007.

Alum Rock Union Elementary School District. "Strategic Communications Plan." San Jose, CA, September 2009. www.arusd.org/202510616123950867 /lib/202510616123950867/STRATEGIC_COMMUNICATIONS_PLAN 2009-2010.pdf (accessed March 22, 2010).

Annunzio, Susan Lucia. *Contagious Success: Spreading High Performance throughout Your Organization*. New York: Penguin, 2004.

Arnsparger, Arleen, Adam Kernan-Schloss, Andy Plattner, and Sylvia Soholt. "Building Community Support for Schools: A Practical Guide to Strategic Communications." Education Commission of the States, Denver, June 1997. www.eric.ed.gov/PDFS/ED410606.pdf (accessed July 8, 2010).

Azcoitia, Carlos. "A New Vision of 'Community Schools.'" *Catalyst Chicago* (September 2005). www.catalyst-chicago.org/news/index.php?item=1638&cat=20 (accessed August 9, 2010).

Baker, Peter. "Responding to Spill, Obama Mixes Regret with Resolve." *New York Times*, May 27, 2010.

Barth, Roland. Foreword to *Leading and Learning*, by Fred Steven Brill. Portland, ME: Stenhouse, 2008.

———. "A Personal Vision of Schooling." *Phi Delta Kappan* 70, no. 7 (March 1990): 512–16.

Berg, Bill. "Mind over Media." Media Educational Services, Addison, IL, 1990.

Black, Lisa. "Antioch District Decides against Book Ban." *Chicago Tribune*, June 23, 2009.

Boston Public Schools. "Strategic Communications." Boston, 2006.

Boyatzis, Richard, and Annie McKee. *Resonant Leadership*. Boston: Harvard Business School Press, 2005.

Brill, Fred Steven. *Leading and Learning*. Portland, ME: Stenhouse, 2008.

Bryk, Anthony, and Barbara Schneider. *Trust in Schools: A Core Resource for Improvement*. New York: Russell Sage Foundation, 2002.

Burns, Greg. "Education Secretary Arne Duncan Counting on Business Leaders to Help Push through School Reforms." *Chicago Tribune*, July 6, 2009.

Bushaw, William J., and John A. McNee. "Americans Speak Out: Are Educators and Policy Makers Listening? The 41st Annual Phi Delta Kappa/Gallup Poll of the Public's Attitudes toward the Public Schools." *Phi Delta Kappan* 91, no. 1 (September 2009): 8–23.

Butler, Kevin. "Tweeting Your Own Horn." *District Administration* (February 2010). www.districtadministration.com/viewarticle.aspx?articleid=2281 (accessed March 23, 2010).

Casey, Maura J. "So Is That Like an A?" *New York Times*, February 14, 2008.

Childress, Stacey. "Six Lessons for Pursuing Excellence and Equity at Scale." *Phi Delta Kappan* 91, no. 3 (November 2009): 13–18.

Colorado Association of School Boards. "Public Engagement in Five Colorado School Communities: Report to the Kettering Foundation." Denver, July 15, 2003.

Covey, Stephen M. R., with Rebecca R. Merrill. *The Speed of Trust: The One Thing That Changes Everything*. New York: Free Press, 2006.

Covey, Stephen R. *The 8th Habit: From Effectiveness to Greatness*. New York: Free Press, 2004.

———. *The 7 Habits of Highly Effective People: Powerful Lessons in Personal Change*. New York: Free Press, 1989.

Dainton, Marianne, and Elaine D. Zelley. *Applying Communication Theory for Professional Life*. Thousand Oaks, CA: Sage, 2005.

Decker, Larry E., and Virginia A. Decker. *Engaging Families and Communities: Pathways to Educational Success*. Fairfax, VA: National Community Education Association, 2002.

Deford, Frank. "The Rabbit Hunter." *Sports Illustrated*, January 26, 1981.

Diebel, Alice. "Public Engagement in Five Colorado School Communities: A Report from the Colorado Association of School Boards." *Connections 2007* (annual newsletter of the Kettering Foundation). www.kettering.org/foundation_programs/public_education/public_engagement_in_five_colorado_school_communities (accessed June 2, 2010).

DuFour, Richard, Rebecca DuFour, Robert Eaker, and Thomas Many. *Learning by Doing: A Handbook for Professional Learning Communities at Work*. Bloomington, IN: Solution Tree, 2006.

Elmira City School District. "Communication Plan 2007–08." Elmira, NY. www.elmiracityschools.com/uploadeddocs/07.08.communication.plan.pdf (accessed March 22, 2010).

Fiore, Douglas J. *School-Community Relations*. Larchmont, NY: Eye on Education, 2002.

Freeman, Donald. *Towards a Descriptive Theory of Teacher Learning and Change.* Brattleboro, VT: Center for Teacher Education, Training and Research, School for International Training, 1999.

Garvey, Georgia. "Evanston Goes Web Route for Budget Help." *Chicago Tribune*, December 30, 2009.

Glasser, William. *The Control Theory Manager.* New York: HarperCollins, 1994.

———. *The Quality School: Managing Students without Coercion.* 2nd ed. New York: Harper Perennial, 1992.

———. *Schools without Failure.* New York: Perennial Library, Harper & Row, 1975.

Grunwald Associates LLC, in cooperation with the National School Boards Association. "Creating and Connecting/Research and Guidelines on Online Social—and Educational—Networking." National School Boards Association, Alexandria, VA, July 2007. www.nsba.org/SecondaryMenu/TLN/Creatingand Connecting.aspx (accessed August 5, 2010).

Harris, Rebecca. "I Have Somewhere to Go." *Catalyst Chicago* (January 2010). www.catalyst-chicago.org/news/index.php?item=2620&cat=32 (accessed May 27, 2010).

Hechinger, John, and Suzanne Sataline. "For More Mayors, School Takeovers Are a No-Brainer." *Wall Street Journal*, March 12, 2009.

Kaplan, Robert S., and Dylan N. Miyake. "The Balanced Scorecard." *School Administrator* 67, no. 2 (February 2010): 10–15.

Kennedy, Kathleen. "Oklahoma City Public Schools: Communications Strategic Plan 2008–2009." www.okcps.k12.ok.us/Communications (accessed February 25, 2010).

Kernan-Schloss, Adam, and Andy Plattner. "Talking to the Public About Public Schools." *Educational Leadership* 56, no. 2 (October 1998): 18–22.

Kidwell, David, and Bob Goldsborough. "Wheaton Warrenville School Board to Release Records, Illinois Supreme Court." *Chicago Tribune*, May 22, 2009.

Kouzes, Jim, and Barry Posner. "The Five Practices of Exemplary Leadership." In *The Jossey-Bass Reader on Educational Leadership.* 2nd ed. San Francisco: Wiley, 2007.

LaFee, Scott. "Transparency." *School Administrator* 66, no. 1 (January 2009): 10–15.

Langford, Barry, and Frank Hunsicker. "An Integrated View of the Relationship between the Organization and the Environment." *Business Quest* 1, no. 1 (1995): 1–10.

Lending, Tod, and David Mrazek. *The Principal Story.* Chicago: Ethno Pictures, Nomadic Pictures, Wallace Foundation, 2009.

Leonard, Sally. "Opportunities Lost: A Few Pointers on PR from an Educational Marketer." *Education Week* 23, no. 11 (November 12, 2003): 29–30.

Marzano, Robert J., Timothy Waters, and Brian A. McNulty. *School Leadership that Works: From Research to Results.* Alexandria, VA: ASCD, 2005.

McLaughlin, Milbrey W., and Joan E. Talbert. *Building School-Based Teacher Learning Communities: Professional Strategies to Improve Student Achievement.* New York: Teachers College Press, 2006.

Meier, Deborah. *In Schools We Trust.* Boston: Beacon, 2002.

Mendelsohn, Jennifer. "Honey, Don't Bother Mommy. I'm Too Busy Building My Brand." *New York Times,* March 12, 2010.

Mizrahi, Jennifer Laszlo, and Talton Gibson. "Winning Advocacy." *School Administrator* 61, no. 3 (March 2004): 10–13.

Moore, Lynn. "Superintendents Taking Case to People—through Videotape (Videos)." *Muskegon (Michigan) News,* January 24, 2010.

Odden, Allan, and Lawrence Picus. *School Finance: A Policy Perspective.* New York: McGraw-Hill, 2008.

Porterfield, Kitty, and Meg Carnes. *Why School Communication Matters: Strategies from PR Professionals.* Lanham, MD: Rowman & Littlefield Education, 2008.

Reed, Diane E., Allison J. Armstrong, and Renee A. Williams. "Laptops and Communication Lessons." *School Administrator* 62, no. 7 (August 2005). www.aasa.org/SchoolAdministratorArticle.aspx?id=8468 (accessed August 3, 2010).

Reeves, Douglas. *The Daily Disciplines of Leadership: How to Improve Student Achievement, Staff Motivation, and Personal Organization.* San Francisco: Jossey-Bass, 2002.

———. "Making Strategic Planning Work." *Educational Leadership* 65, no. 4 (December 2007/January 2008): 86–87.

Robinson, L. Oliver. "Combating the Rumor Mill through a Grapevine." *School Administrator* 67, no. 1 (January 2010). www.aasa.org/SchoolAdministratorArticle.aspx?id=11048 (accessed March 23, 2010).

Rockwood School District. "Comprehensive Communications Plan 2009–2010." Rockwood Communications, Wildwood, MO, 2009. www.rockwood.k12.mo.us/communications/Downloads/Comprehensive%20Communications%20Plan%202009-2010.pdf (accessed February 26, 2010).

Shirky, Clay. *Here Comes Everybody: The Power of Organizing without Organizations.* New York: Penguin, 2008.

Skokie Review (Illinois). "Stingy Tax Caps Impact 73.5 Levy," November 16, 2009.

Skokie (Illinois) School District 73½. "Community Digest." Fall 2009. www.sd735.org/education/components/scrapbook/default.php?sectiondetailid=2647& (accessed October 12, 2010).

Soholt, Sylvia. "Public Engagement: Lessons from the Front." *Educational Leadership* 56, no. 2 (October 1998): 22–23.

Spiegel, Peter. "Report: Air Force Flubbed Missile Checks." *Los Angeles Times,* October 20, 2007.

Spillane, James P., and John B. Diamond. *Distributive Leadership in Practice.* New York: Teachers College Press, 2007.

Springfield Public Schools. "Strategic Communications Plan." Springfield Public Schools, Springfield, MA, March 2009. www.sps.springfield.ma.us/deptsites

/communications/content/SPSStrategicCommunicationsPlan.pdf (accessed August 9, 2010).

Stiggins, Richard J., Judith A. Arter, Jan Chappuis, and Stephen Chappuis. *Classroom Assessment for Student Learning*. Portland, OR: Assessment Training Institute, 2004.

Toone, Trent. "Creativity, Imagination Churned Out through Teachers' 'Machine.'" *Ogden Standard-Examiner* (Utah), December 23, 2009.

Tschannen-Moran, Megan. *Trust Matters: Leadership for Successful Schools*. San Francisco: Jossey-Bass, 2004.

Twin Rivers Unified School District. "2008–2009 Communications Plan." North Highlands, CA, 2008.

Wall Street Journal. "Gulf News Urges Reporters to Tone Down Dubai Coverage," December 24, 2009.

Warren, Jim. "Harrison School District Gets Award." *Lexington Herald-Leader* (Kentucky), December 5, 2009.

Weissbourd, Richard. *The Parents We Mean to Be: How Well-Intentioned Adults Undermine Children's Moral and Emotional Development*. Boston: Houghton Mifflin Harcourt, 2009.

Wenger, Etienne. *Communities of Practice: Learning, Meaning and Identity*. New York: Cambridge University Press, 1998.

Westmoreland, Helen, Heidi M. Rosenberg, M. Elena Lopez, and Heather Weiss. "Seeing Is Believing: Promising Practices for How School Districts Promote Family Engagement." Harvard Family Research Project and National Parent Teacher Association (PTA), issue brief, July 2009. http://pta.org/Issue_Brief-SeeingisBelieving.pdf (accessed June 3, 2010).

Wheatley, Margaret. "Goodbye, Command and Control." *Leader to Leader* (July 1997).

Zand, D. E. *The Leadership Triad: Knowledge, Trust, and Power*. New York: Oxford University Press, 1997.

INDEX

administrators, communication with, 39
advocacy, 25–34; media and, 32–33
alignment, of goals/values and communications, 51–68; definition of, 51
alumni, communication with, 41, 124–25
Alum Rock (CA) United Elementary District, 39
Annunzio, Susan Lucia, 29
Arnett, Jeffrey, 86
Arnsparger, Arleen, 97
Arter, Judith, 37–38
assessment, and strategic communications plan, 98–100, 153–55
Atlanta Public Schools, 57
audience, 37–50; characteristics of, 38–43; internal versus external, 38–39, 38*t*; research on, 43
audio communications, 43–44; student-generated, 46
audit, of communications, 98–100, 153–55
automated telephone calls, 45
Avossa, Robert, 58
Azcoitia, Carlos, 61–62

Bagin, Rich, 4
Baker, Peter, 163n13
balanced-scorecard approach, 57
Barrington (IL) District 220, 86, 92, 92*f*
Barth, Roland S., vii–viii, xv, 60, 70
Beaverton (OR) School District, 46, 47*f*
behavior: as communication, 58–67; and credibility, 78–83
Berg, Bill, 32, 80–81
blogs, 88, 90, 92–94, 95*b*
BLTs. *See* building leadership teams
board, communication with, 40, 40*b*; teams for, 83
body language, as communication, 60
Boston Public Schools, 38, 111
Brill, Fred, 23–24, 61
Bryk, Anthony, 13
budget issues. *See* financial reporting; tax levies
building-based communications, 44–45
building leadership teams (BLTs), 65

Carnes, Meg, 25, 33
Carr, Nora, 80
CASB. *See* Colorado Association of School Boards

Casey, Maura, 10
channels, of communication, 43–49; coordination of, 105; technological changes and, 85–87
Chappuis, Jan, 37–38
Chappuis, Steve, 37–38
Charlotte-Mecklenburg (NC) Schools, 58, 59f, 80
Childress, Stacey, 20
clarity, and communications plan, 105
collaboration, and good communication, 113
Colorado Association of School Boards (CASB), 64, 79, 116
commitments: and good communication, 113–14; standing by, 79
communication, xiii–xvii; and audience, 37–50; audit of, 98–100, 153–55; channels of, 43–49; details for inclusion in, 6, 11, 31, 37–40, 49–50; goals and values and, 51–68; good, model of, 111–16; importance of, xiii, 1–34; political savvy and, 28; recommendations for, 35–107; show don't tell, 69–75; on tax issues, 26–28. *See also* strategic communications plan
communities of interest, 88
community: communication with, 125–28; engaging, 62–64; values and, 61–62; vision statement on, 144–45
community leaders, communication with, 41
Complete Communications Inc., 149, 153
consolidation, standing by commitments and, 79
conversations, technological changes and, 88–90
cooperation, and communications plan, 105

Covey, Stephen M. R., 20, 77–78, 163n3
Covey, Stephen R.: on emotional bank account, 13–14, 158n5; on expectations, 66
credibility, 77–84; definition of, 77–78; and financial reporting, 7
crisis, communication in, 80–82, 106–7, 163n13
critical thinking, vision statement on, 146
critics, engaging, 29–32

Daily Five literacy program, 72–73
dashboard approach, 58, 59f, 70
deadlines, and communications plan, 106
DeFeciani, Kelly, 92–93
Deming, W. Edward, 16
Diebel, Alice, 64
differentiation, of communication, 37–38; examples of, 117–38; and messages, 55
disclosure, 3; of whole story, 80–82
distributive leadership, 20
District 54, Schaumburg (IL), 16–17, 19–20, 83
District 73½, Skokie (IL): characteristics of, xv; development of mission statement for, 52–54, 53f, 139–47; differentiated communications from, 129–38; tax levy communications from, 117–28; trust in, 21
District 145, Freeport (IL), 71
District 220, Barrington (IL), 86, 92, 92f

elevator speech, 55
Elmira (NY) City School District, 41, 102
e-mail, as communication channel, 44, 47

emphasis, and communication, 72–73
engagement: with community, 62–64; with critics, 29–32; and good communication, 115–16; and persuasion, 70–71; with public, 91–94; with staff, 64–66; with teachers, 94–95
Evanston, IL, 91
examples, in communication, 74
expectations, clarifying, 66

Facebook, 95b
facts: versus assertions, 69–75; and story, 71–72
families. See parents
feedback, 22–24
financial reporting, 5–7; and advocacy, 26; messaging on, 54–55
Fiore, Douglas J., 6
Flickr, 95b
Freedom of Information Act (FOIA), 30
Freeport (IL) District 145, 71

Gibson, Talton, 69
Glasser, William, 16
goals: and communications, 51–68; exemplifying, 58–67; identification and articulation of, 52–54; progress toward, reporting on, 57–58; and strategic communications plan, 100–101
Gorman, Peter, 80

Haley, Julia, 16, 29
Hall, Beverly, 57
Hanson, Linda, 17
Harvard Family Research Project, 115
Highwood-Highland Park (IL) School District 111, 79
Honeoye Falls-Lima (NY) Central School District, 22–23

honesty: and credibility, 79–80; and trust, 18–22

interpersonal communications, 45

Kernan-Schloss, Adam, 63, 97
Kettering Foundation, 64
Knight, Bob, xiii
Kouzes, Jim, 37

Lake Mills (IA) Community School, 10, 11f
Lafayette, CA, 61
language: in communication campaigns, 27; and differentiation, 42–43
leadership: distributive, 20; vision statement on, 142–43
Leonard, Sally, 58
LinkedIn, 96b
listening: and credibility, 82–83; respect and, 29b; teachers and, 56; and trust, 23–24
local businesses, communication with, 41

marketing research, 43
Marquis, Trinette, 31
Marzano, Robert, 64
McLaughlin, Milbrey, 65
McNulty, Brian, 64
media: and advocacy, 32–33; as channel, 45–46; communication with, 41
Meier, Deborah, 13
messages, development of, 54–55, 70–71
messengers, teachers as, 55–57
microsites, 42, 46
Mid-continent Research for Education and Learning, 162n19
mission statements, development of, 52–54, 53f, 139–47

mistakes, communication about, 18*b*
Mizrahi, Jennifer Laszlo, 69
mommy blogs, 88
multimedia, 73–74
MySpace, 95*b*

National Parent-Teacher Association, 115
National School Public Relations Association (NSPRA), 31, 80, 83, 98
National School Reform Faculty, 162n19
Navis, Irene, 77
newsletters, technological changes and, 85–87
9/9/9 Outreach Program, 62
No Child Left Behind Act, 9
NSPRA. *See* National School Public Relations Association
nutrition issues, 30–31

Obama, Barack, 163n13
Oklahoma City Public Schools, 103
Olsen, Jason, 90
one-on-one communications, 45
openness: and credibility, 79–80; with media, 32; and trust, 18–22
Orcutt, Karen, 83
Orono (MN) Public Schools, 83

parents: communication with, 39, 117–21, 136–38; good communication and, 111–12; as internal versus external audience, 38–39; and nutrition concerns, 30–31; teacher communications with, 149–51; and technology, 90; and whole story, 81–82
passive voice, 163n13
PBIS. *See* Positive Behavior Intervention System
Peel (Ontario, Canada) District School Board, 42

persuasion, 70–71
phone trees, 45
Plattner, Andy, 63, 97
PLC. *See* professional learning community
political savvy, 28
Porter, Frank, 32, 64
Porterfield, Kitty, 25, 33
Positive Behavior Intervention System (PBIS), 55
Posner, Barry, 37
Powell, Griff, 28, 40*b*, 79
print communications, 43–44
professional learning community (PLC), 53, 64–65, 153, 162n19
progress review: and amendments, 103–4; and strategic communications plan, 102–3
public: and advocacy, 25–34; engaging, 91–94; and funding, 26; right to know, 3–12
Purcell, Kerry, 65–66

Rafferty, Ed, 17, 19–20, 33, 83
Reeves, Douglas, 51
research, on audience, 43
respect: behavior and, 61; in communication, 29–30; with media, 32
responsibility, and communications plan, 105
risk-taking: discouraging behavior and, 60; and trust, 20
Robinson, L. Oliver, 93
Rockwood, MO, 100–101, 112–13
rumors, coping with, 89–90, 92

Salt Lake City School District, 90
Schaumburg (IL) District 54, 16–17, 19–20, 83
Schneider, Barbara, 13
Shenendohowa (NY) Central Schools, 92–94
Shirky, Clay, 85, 87, 94

Skokie (IL) District 73½. *See* District 73½, Skokie (IL)
social networking, 47, 87–96, 102
social media, 47; and changes in communication, 87–96; keeping up with, 90–91; tools for, 95–96
Soholt, Sylvia, 97
Spillane, James, 20
Springfield, MA, 100
Spry Community Links High School (Chicago), 61–62
Spry Elementary School (Chicago), 61–62
staff: communication with, 38–40, 121–24; data on, 7–9; engaging, 64–66; media and, 33; and technology, 90
stakeholders: and articulation of values, 52; characteristics of, 38–43; as communities of interest, 88; engaging, 64–66; good communication and, 111; managing voices of, 66–67; voice for, 16–17
Stewart, Nancy, 94–95
Stiggins, Richard, 37–38
strategic communications plan, 97–107; amendments to, 103–4; characteristics of, 114; and crisis, 106–7; management and, 105–6
Streedain, Dick, 18–19, 62
students: achievement data on, 9–10; communication with, 39; demographic data on, 7–9; displaying work of, 72
superintendent's communication council, 83

Tafel, Linda, 29*b*
Talbert, Joan, 65
tax levies: communication about, 6, 26–28, 117–28; political savvy and, 28
teachers: communication with, 39–40, 129–35; and Daily Five literacy program, 72–73; engaging, 94–95; and family communications, 149–51; as messengers, 55–57; and trust, 21*b*
technology, 85–96
telephone communications, 45
time, and communication, 5–6
translation, issues in, 42
transparency. *See* openness
trust, 13–24; building, 15–24; emotional bank account, 13–14, 158n5; level of, assessment of, 14–15
Tschannen-Moran, Megan, 4, 13–14, 18
Tufte, Edward, 43, 160n12
Twin Rivers (CA) Unified School District, xiii, 31–32, 40, 45, 63–64
Twitter, 95*b*

values: and communications, 51–68; exemplifying, 58–67; and good communication, 114–15; identification and articulation of, 52–54
variety, and communication, 73–74
Venezky, Dina, 89–90
video communications, 43–44; student-generated, 46
virtual communication board, 104
vision statements: ambition in, 112–16; development of, 52–54, 53*f*, 139–47

Waters, Timothy, 64
websites: as communication channel, 44, 46, 47*f*; language issues and, 42; on student achievements, 10, 11*f*; student work displayed on, 72
Weissbourd, Richard, 56, 111–12
Wheatley, Margaret, 19
Wikipedia, 95*b*–96*b*
Wynne, Michael, 18, 81

Ylisela, James, Jr., 104
YouTube, 92, 92*f*, 95*b*

ABOUT THE AUTHORS

Dr. Vicki Gunther is on the faculty of National-Louis University, Chicago, Illinois, where she teaches graduate students who aspire to be principals and school superintendents. She is well grounded in the practical application of educational theory and research and enjoys the opportunity to share her perspective at the university level.

Dr. Gunther has been a public school teacher, administrator, principal, and superintendent. She has cultivated leadership at all levels, mentored new teachers and administrators, and designed staff development programs on best practices in curriculum, instruction, and assessment. She is keenly aware of local politics, community expectations, and the need for school leaders to build and nurture relationships with students, parents, staff members, and the community.

James McGowan has operated a small communications company in Skokie, Illinois, for twenty-four years, in partnership with his wife, Sharon. He has planned, written, designed, and executed communications for school districts, nonprofits, associations, and corporations. He also has worked as a newspaper reporter and copy editor.

McGowan served for eight years on his local public school board, the last five as president. During that time, he learned much about the field of education and about the critical role communication plays in the success of schools.

Kate Donegan is the superintendent of a school district in Skokie, Illinois, where more than 50 percent of the student population comes from homes where a language other than English is spoken. Donegan has a strong background in special education and school finance. Along with coauthor

McGowan, Donegan conducted the district's first communication audit and developed a three-year communications plan to seek new and better ways to gain input from parent and community members and keep them informed of district initiatives. Prior to becoming the superintendent, Donegan was a special education resource teacher and served as the middle school principal in the district. She has three young children, two who currently attend the district where she serves as superintendent.

Made in the USA
Columbia, SC
30 May 2023